Stitches and Seams

Stitches and Seams

Essential Sewing Skills for the
Beginner Sewist, Tailor, and DIY Crafter

Valeria Carrandi Macías

Stitches and Seams

Essential Sewing Skills for the Beginner Sewist, Tailor, and DIY Crafter

Valeria Carrandi Macías

Project editor: Maggie Yates
Project manager: Lisa Brazieal
Marketing coordinator: Katie Walker
Cover design, cover production: Aren Straiger
Interior design and layout: Kim Scott, Bumpy Design

ISBN: 979-8-88814-029-1
1st Edition (1st printing, October 2023)

Rocky Nook Inc.
1010 B Street, Suite 350
San Rafael, CA 94901
USA

www.rockynook.com

Distributed in the UK and Europe by Publishers Group UK
Distributed in the U.S. and all other territories by Publishers Group West

Library of Congress Control Number: 2023933262

Printed in China.

To my father, who always knew.

"El saber no ocupa espacio."
"Knowledge takes up no space."

To my husband,
for feeding my tummy and creative soul
while writing this book.

And to you, aspiring sewist,
thank you for making me a part
of your sewing journey.

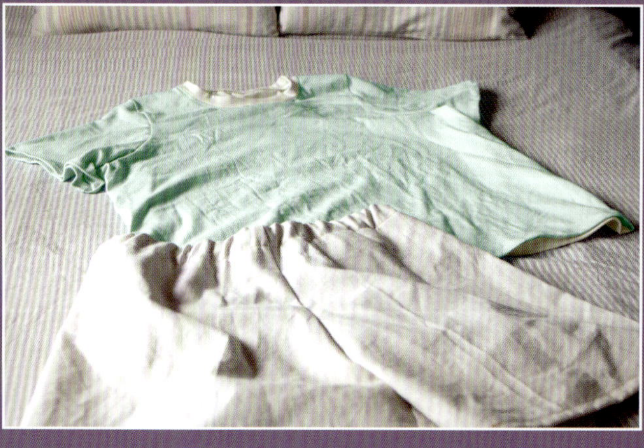

TABLE OF CONTENTS

SINGER Confidence

Introduction

DISCOVERING THE ART OF SEWING

As creative people, most of our origin stories go back as far as our childhood—starting with DIY pasta necklaces for our mother, "Best Dad Award" frames, or make-shift Halloween outfits—and mine is no different. I took every painting, drawing, pottery, and artsy after-school class my grandmother could find me, and even though I liked most of them, nothing really scratched my itch.

During my teenage-angst phase I lost sight of all creative endeavors while I was trying to figure out who I was. But while searching for something to call mine, I started craving a creative outlet, something original and out of the box. But I had no idea what that could be. We are talking about 2007, so the internet wasn't such a big place to go and find inspiration. There was no Instagram, no Pinterest, and the world of blogging was nonexistent to my knowledge. Nevertheless, I searched for fashion courses near my town and a flame was sparked.

I enrolled in a year-long pattern drafting and sewing course. Early Saturday mornings, my mom would drive me across the city to learn how to construct a garment with my own measurements, and my dad bought me my first sewing machine, which I still use to this day.

Muslins were sewn, terminology was noted, and a solid basis on pattern making was set. Sadly, it wasn't enough for me to make my own clothing at that point. It wasn't until I discovered the wondrous world of online home sewing patterns that I had a huge mindset shift into the possibilities of sewing everything I wear. That's the exact turning point where I truly got good at sewing—by trying new things, understanding pattern making, figuring out pattern modifications, and getting good results in my garments and sewing projects.

I must admit my background in textile design (which was my major) helped me in further understanding what one can do in terms of fashion, creative design, textile use, and resources when sewing. That being said, I will use them as a backbone while writing so you'll get a wider scope of what can be achieved in garment making.

What I intend to do with this book is give you the tools and building blocks to kickstart your sewing journey, to build confidence enough to sew your first garment, knowing what to expect and how to tackle any challenges. I am convinced that by having good foundation blocks, we can build anything in our imagination. Sewing basics are always the same whether it is for a pillowcase or a wedding dress. The sky's the limit.

There is much to learn beyond what I share here with you; the creative field and the sewing universe is vast with much to give. Use this book as a starting point and reference back to it as much as needed.

I hope it sparks a flame in you, as my early discoveries did for me.

BENEFITS OF LEARNING TO SEW

True Connection: Knowing how much effort and time it takes to create a piece of clothing has truly changed my perception of owning things. I now see these items as highly valuable, worth caring for and mending. We wear sewn items of clothing daily—that's a special bond right there.

Well-Fitting Garments: Making garments with your own body measurements is the basis of home sewing, which means they mostly fit very well (sometimes they need a bit of adjustment). Even if it's not clothing, your sewing projects will be made to your own requirements, fulfilling your unique needs. Never have I felt the peace of mind and body in a store as I have in my sewing room.

Delayed Gratification: Sewing takes time and effort, which is why the end result tastes much sweeter—because of the effort it took to get there to enjoy the results.

Keeps Your Hands off Scrolling: Am I the only one craving connection to something beyond my phone? Sewing is a perfect activity other than screen time.

Fun "Me" Time: Sewing can be quite therapeutic and meditative—once I get into a rhythm I find that my creative juices start flowing; by "creative" I don't mean only of the crafty nature—it is a moment of introspection that helps me bake new ideas, solve problems, and feel at ease.

Community: I enjoy sharing knowledge, techniques, tips, and tutorials. No one is as fast as a crafter to spill their tips. I've learned more from inspiring people than I ever did at school.

SEWING PRINCIPLES

For each sewing project in this book, I'll show you step by step how to complete it. While those instructions are of a more technical nature, I also want to share my top-of-mind sewing principles that have helped me make my sewing more manageable and enjoyable. These are not hard-and-fast rules, but simple, friendly advice. The more you sew, the more you'll realize that you already came up with your own principles through experience.

- **Make It Your Own**

  Try these techniques and adapt them to your needs. There is always more than one way to achieve neat results. This applies to this book and to life. You never know—you might be onto something new by doing it your way.

- **Become Great at Searching and Questioning**

  There is *so* much information out there. When facing a challenge, chances are someone has already triumphed over it and made a tutorial about it, which comes in really handy when sewing new things. But learn to question methods, resources, and techniques. Exercise critical thinking in choosing which sources to consume.

- **Take Notes**

  I've made the crass mistake of thinking I'll remember how many inches or centimeters I added to a pattern, or the step by step of an awesome tutorial online. Spoiler alert: I never do. Write it down. Make all the notes. Your future self will thank you when you want to repeat making the exact same garment; in the process you'll get an awesome sewing diary where you can see all your progress.

- **Baby Steps**

  Yes, there's the occasional success story of "person who has never sewn creates wedding gown in two days." In reality, inching your way toward more and greater challenges is way more feasible. This mindset also applies to supplies. To begin, you don't need *all* the supplies nor the most advanced sewing machine. Start small and grow with each project.

- **To Stitch Is to Unstitch**

  It used to unnerve me every time I had to rip a seam. I've grown to accept it as part of the process, just like erasing when sketching. We are only human, and we get distracted. We don't always have a perfectly chill sewing session. So take a deep breath, grab your seam ripper, and keep it moving.

- **Master the Iron Press**

  Truth is, if the instruction says to iron press, it is worth doing. Yes, it is an extra step, and yes, I also thought it was useless until I started doing so and it changed my finished garments. You are just one press away from creating a neat-looking garment.

- **Gentle Over Brutal**

  Maybe it's just me, but I used to skip lunch or hold it in for hours just so I could finish a garment. Needless to say, my sewing sessions were filled with stress. Enjoy the ride, take the break, pause and pick it up another day. I've made more mistakes by working tirelessly, filled with frustration and hurry than by being slower but steady.

- **Let Go of the "Should Haves"**

  More often than not we want the bias binding lining, the matching overlocker thread, the perfectly crisp button up—but every once in a while we need a quick fix and we can't be bothered with matching thread—and that is perfectly okay. Don't get discouraged by sewing purists. The person at the machine is you. You do you!

- **Practice Makes Progress**

  We are all familiar with the saying "practice makes perfect," but even with all my years in sewing I still have a long way to go toward perfection. I aim for progress: to be better at my craft than I was a year ago, a decade ago. Progress is measurable, whereas perfection will always leave room to subjective opinion.

- **Value the Process as Much as the Result**

  This is the ultimate life principle, even beyond sewing. The journey is the reward. Learn to appreciate the work you put into it: This mindset will make sewing a lifelong friend.

CHAPTER 1

Fabric

I want to start at the very top. The main ingredient for sewing (besides the desire) is fabric. Maybe it's my inner textile designer talking, but I believe fabric is the component that makes or breaks a sewing project. I cannot tell you how many times I've had horrible end results by choosing the wrong fabric, and how many times I have created a much better garment by choosing the right one.

The good news is, you don't need to major in textile studies for this—I've got you. In this section we'll go over the basic information you'll need to have to really know fabric. This, plus diving into fabric stores, touching all the fabrics and experimenting with them will make you a fabric master.

WHAT IS FABRIC?

We are all familiar with fabric. We wear it for fashion to express our unique selves, we wear it for need when protecting our body from extreme weather, we sleep in sheets made of fabric, sit on our car seats made of textiles, and decorate every corner of our homes with it. I dare say, fabric is as used and as important as food.

If you are anything like me, the main reason you want to sew clothes is because of fabric, its colors, textures, and feel—so knowing how it is created and how to differentiate the various types comes in super handy at the moment of choosing the fabric for your next sewing project.

Fabric is well known as an end result, but how is it made? The process consists of three main components: fibers, thread, and weave.

FIBERS

The base for all fabric is fibers. Fibers are a long and narrow filament that must have resistance and elasticity to be properly transformed into thread, then fabric.

Originally, fibers came from the natural world and were divided in two categories: plant based like cotton and linen; and animal based like wool and silk.

It wasn't until 1885 that the first artificial fiber was created: rayon. Looking to emulate silk, which was the most expensive fabric at that time, rayon was similar to the touch but faster and cheaper to produce. Its raw material is cotton lint or wood, and by dissolving it in chemical solutions a new fiber is born.

After artificial fibers, synthetic fibers came to be. In synthetic fibers, the raw material is a

combination of monomers that create polymers, so no natural resources are mined. It is all man-made.

From that point on, textile technology created more and more fibers to reduce cost, yield faster results, be more durable, be eco-conscious, use nanotechnology, you name it—in the 21st century we have fibers and textiles for almost anything.

Here's a list of popular fibers used in clothes and home sewing, along with an image of the fabric each creates. By chemical compound, there are three main groups: protein fibers (which come from animals), cellulose fibers (which come from plants), and synthetic fibers (which come from chemical processing).

PROTEIN FIBERS	CELLULOSE FIBERS	SYNTHETIC
NATURAL		Nylon
Alpaca	Cotton (seed)	Polyester
Angora (angora rabbit)	Linen (stem)	Elastane/Spandex
Silk (silk worm)	Jute (stem)	Acrylic
Wool (sheep)	Hemp (stem)	
Mohair (angora goat)	Ramie (stem)	
Cashmere (goat)		
ARTIFICIAL		
Azlon	Rayon/viscose	
	Tencel/Lyocell	
	Acetate/Triacetate	

PROTEIN FIBERS (NATURAL)

Alpaca

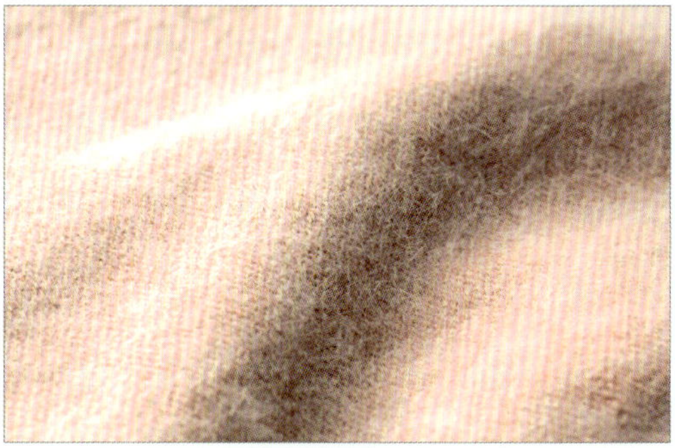

Angora (from the Angora rabbit)

Silk (from the silkworm)

Wool (from sheep)

Mohair (from the Angora goat)

Cashmere (from goats)

CELLULOSE FIBERS (NATURAL)

Cotton

Linen

Jute

Hemp

Ramie

CELLULOSE FIBERS (ARTIFICIAL)

Rayon

Tencel

Acetate

SYNTHETIC FIBERS

Nylon

Polyester

Elastane

Acrylic

THREAD

A group of fibers, twisted together to intermesh, are referred to as thread. To transform fibers into thread, think of the spinning wheel, where fibers are elongated through the wheel and then twisted into the bobbin creating a continuous thread out of tons of tiny, short fibers. Of course, the spinning wheel is the traditional method—the current industry uses the same principle, but at a much bigger scale.

In the case of synthetic fibers, the thread can be produced in a continuous single strand called monofilament, without the need to twist and mesh fibers together; this is similar to silk thread (made of a natural fiber), which is also created with a single strand.

This is how and why blends are created. Twisting together two different fibers to create a new thread diminishes the not-so-ideal characteristics of each fiber and maximizes the desirable ones.

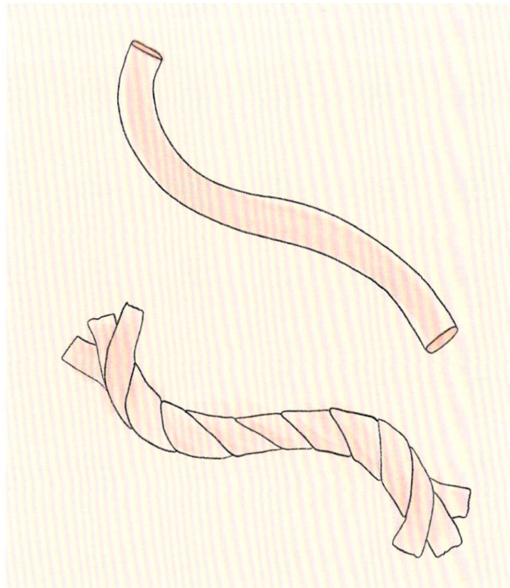

On top, the monofilament has no twist or strands. On bottom, the thread is made of various strands of fibers twisted together.

WEAVE

Back when I was studying textile design at college, after covering the topics of fibers and thread, our first class in the universe of actual fabric was about weaving. That makes perfect sense, even intuitively, because woven fabric is one of the oldest forms of fabric creation. Thus the structure of this type of fabric is the easiest to understand, being a perfect building block to move forward into more complex manufacturing processes.

Woven Fabric

Woven fabric is created with at least two separate strands of yarn/thread. One thread is called the warp. It runs vertically through the fabric, determining its length. These yarns must be resistant and top quality to endure the tension caused by the weave.

The second strand is called the weft. This one goes side to side, horizontally weaving the fabric, and determines the fabric's width. These yarns can be more decorative or less resilient.

Fabric is woven by those two strands interlocking each other perpendicularly.

Woven fabric

TIP My advice to differentiate between strands: The warp is usually heavier at the selvedge. This is to stabilize the fabric while being woven at the loom.

The weft sometimes creates a hairy look from the end of the strands going side to side.

The selvedge edge

Let's take into account that regular woven fabric has no stretch because of the plain weave that interlocks perpendicularly. But, these fabrics can have a bit of give diagonally following the bias (called mechanical stretch); or achieve great stretchiness when the main fibers are blended with elastane.

Different weave patterns create different types of fabrics. The three main weave patterns are plain/tabby, twill, and satin.

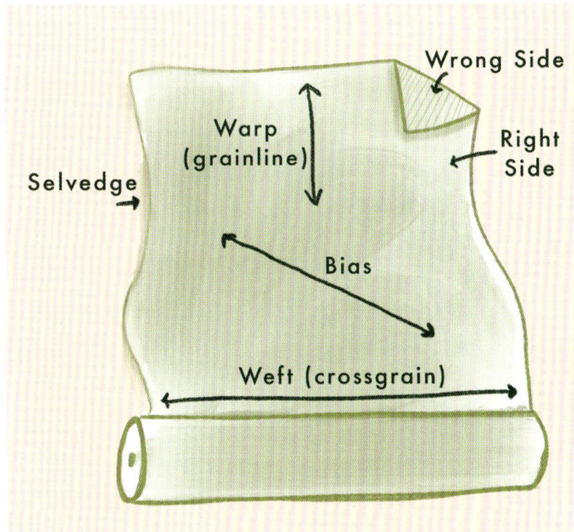

PLAIN/TABBY

- The simplest weave, each warp thread interlocks perpendicularly to one weft thread. 1x1: one over, one under.
- Fabric examples: taffeta, poplin, muslin/calico
- Extended tabby is a variation of the plain weave, where two warp threads interlock with two weft threads. 2x2: two over, two under. This creates a more flexible fabric that is less prone-to-wrinkles due to having fewer interlocked threads per inch.

Plain/Tabby weave

TWILL

- Its main characteristic is creating diagonal lines, because one thread (either on weft or warp) will skip two threads in order to interlock. 2x1: two over, one under.
- Fabric examples: denim, gabardine, tartan, tweed

Twill weave

SATIN

- This weave pattern stands out for leaving a larger section without being interlocked. Because of it, this fabric has more sheen, and a smoother surface. 4x1: four over, one under.
- Fabric examples: charmeuse, sateen

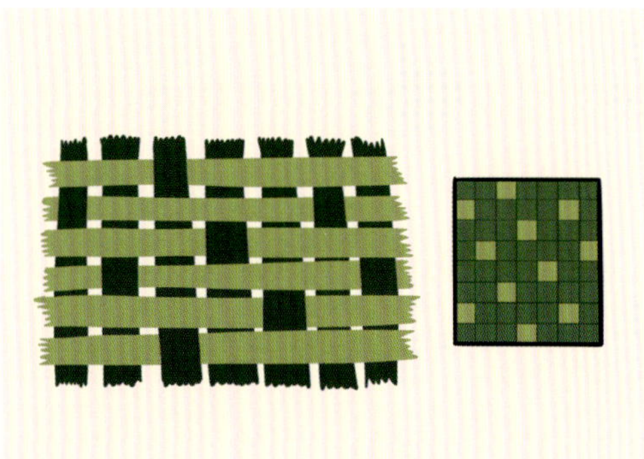

Satin weave

Knit Fabric

Knit is usually the predominant fabric in most wardrobes thanks to its comfort, flexibility, and price point, so knowing knit fabric means opening up possibilities to sew great garments you'll actually wear.

Knit fabric

This type of fabric is created with a process involving one strand of thread or yarn knitting itself. A great example for this would be a scarf, knit with just one ball of yarn and two needles.

The loops created with this technique are what give knit fabric its distinctive stretch. Inside the knit category, we still have two types of knitting looms: weft and warp. Weft knit is a horizontal method, and is commonly used for jersey knit and interlock knit. In warp knit, the loop knits itself while also knitting the warp threads next to it vertically. It requires a more advanced machine, such as a tricot machine or a raschel machine.

Knit fabric is commonly used for its stretchy quality, even while using non-stretchy yarns or threads. This is called mechanical stretch. But elastane can also be added to knit fabric for extra stretch and recovery.

Most of my clothing is made with stretch fabric because it is soft, comfy (it elongates and moves with me), and usually requires less fitting adjustments. If you dive into your wardrobe, I can almost assure you that most of your clothes are made of stretchy materials, too.

When choosing stretch fabric for some of my sewing projects, I keep in mind the following characteristics to decide whether it will suit my design or not: recovery, direction, and percentage of stretchiness.

Recovery: This is the capacity of the fabric to bounce back to its original shape after being stretched. Imagine a wooly sweater. This garment only has mechanical stretch. If you were to wash it and hang it up to dry, chances are

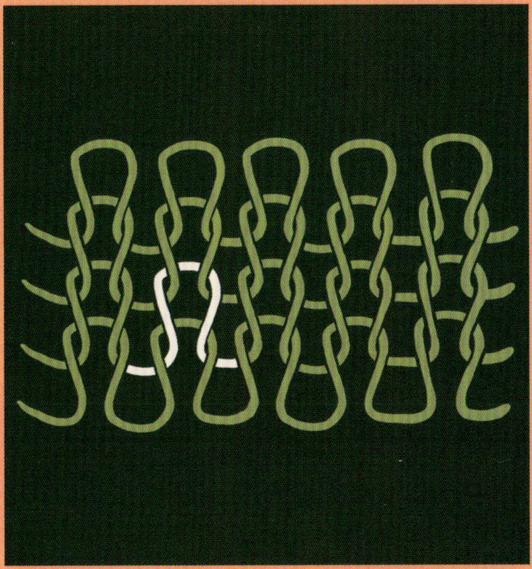

Weft knit

Warp knit

it is going to stretch beyond repair because of the water weight pulling the fibers. Because it has mechanical stretch, it won't recover.

Swimwear with added elastane, on the other hand, will recover to its original shape and size regardless of how much we stretch it. Furthermore, swimwear seems smaller on a hanger, but has lots of room to grow when worn or when in contact with water—and can still bounce back, keeping its original shape.

Direction: In which way can the fabric be stretched? This aspect is divided in two categories:

- **Two-Way Stretch:** When pulled, the fabric stretches left and right, meaning it only stretches in one plane, widthwise, perpendicular to the grainline and selvedge. In the lengthwise direction (parallel to the selvedge), it has little mechanical stretch.

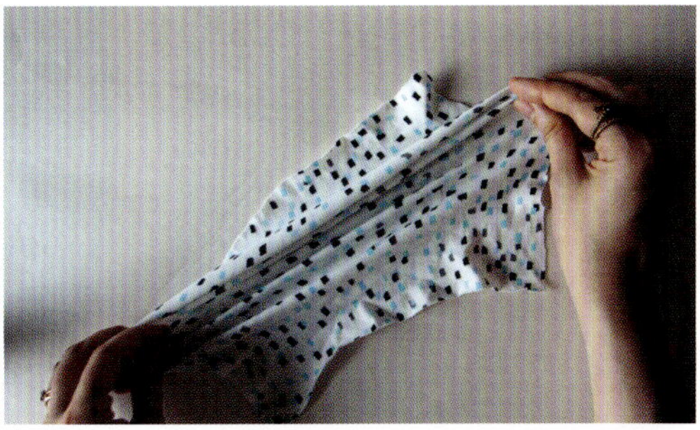

- **Four-Way Stretch:** This kind of fabric can be stretched in two planes, going both up and down and side to side, meaning widthwise and lengthwise. This can be easily tested by stretching the fabric in all directions.

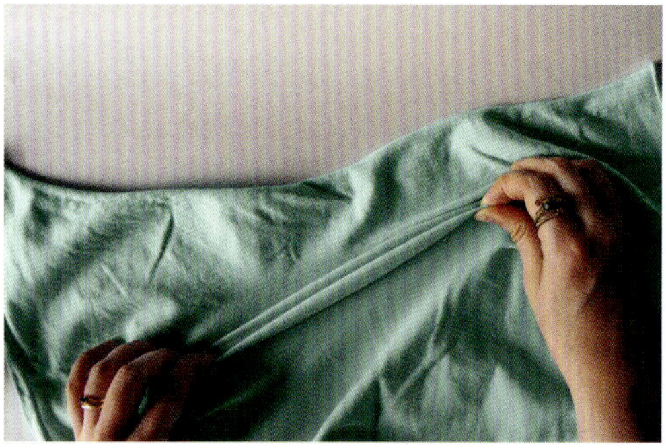

In these images, notice the selvedge runs horizontally at the top (we know from the tiny puncture dots). This fabric can stretch on both planes, resulting in a four-way stretch.

Percentage of stretch: This refers to how stretchy fabric is—how much bigger can it get from its original size when pulled. To figure out this number, do the following:

1. Lay the fabric on your table with the selvedge to the side. (Test the widthwise direction first, that is usually the direction with the most stretch).

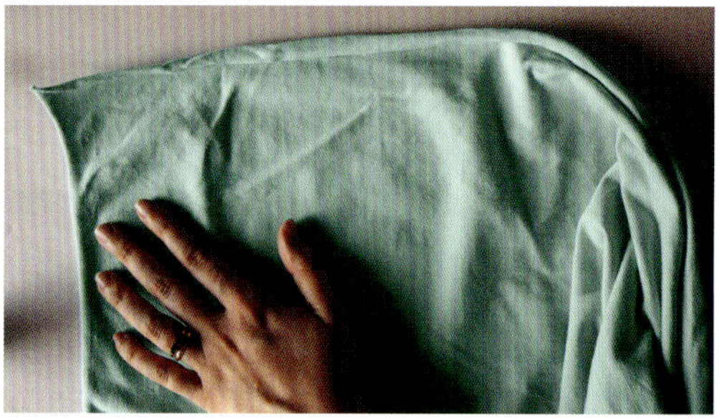

2. Secure one sewing pin. Pin another one 4 in (10 cm) apart from it. (Try to keep them both a little distance from the selvedge).

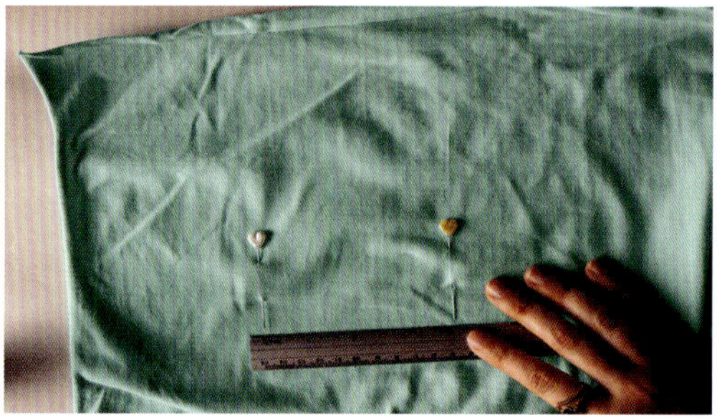

3. Place your ruler at the first pin.
4. Hold it in place and pull the fabric in the opposite direction until you feel resistance, trying not to over stretch it.

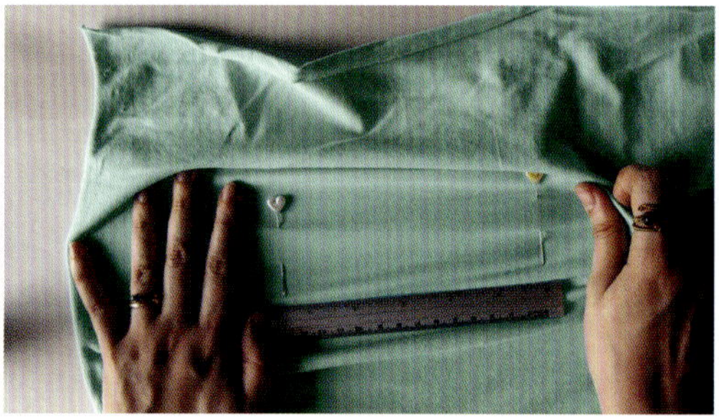

5. Take note of where the second pin lands on the ruler.

6. The formula to find how much stretch a fabric has is the following:

$$\frac{\text{amount fabric stretches}}{\text{original length}} \times 100 = \text{stretch \%}$$

If the original length was 4 inches and it stretched out to 6 inches, then the amount of fabric stretch was 2 inches. Two inches divided by 4 inches = 0.5 inches. When multiplied by 100, the stretch percentage equals 50%.

If a sewing project requires a certain percentage of stretch, use this method and formula to verify that the fabric meets the requirement. Sometimes using a different percentage of stretch than the one recommended can result in an ill-fitting garment. If a sewing project asks for four-way stretch, you can do this exercise for the width and the length to find the percentage for each direction.

Pile Weave

Alright, this is where textiles get a bit more advanced.

Picture both woven and knit fabric as two dimensional, with weave directions on the X and Y axes. Therefore, the pile weave would be a tridimensional fabric, because it has additional thread loops topping the surface of the base weave (Z axis).

Pile weave

Use the reference image at right to picture how the darker thread (pile weave) is taller than the green weft; this way, the pile weave gives extra dimension to the fabric. The pile weave can be kept as loops (as in the drawing), like for towels, or can be cut down and be left open, like for velvet.

Think about a tufted rug. The base canvas is regular woven fabric to which perpendicular threads are added to create the nap, which adds height (and a third dimension) to the original canvas. Pile weave is frequently used for warmth. There are many common examples of fabric with pile weave (also known as nap fabric), including the following:

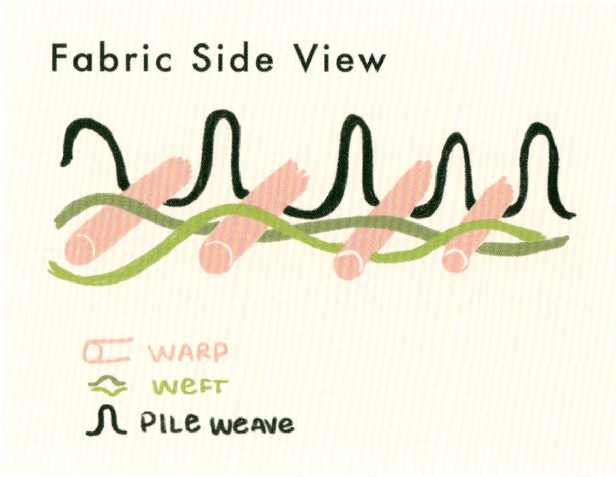

Corduroy

Velvet (commonly a woven base, more expensive)

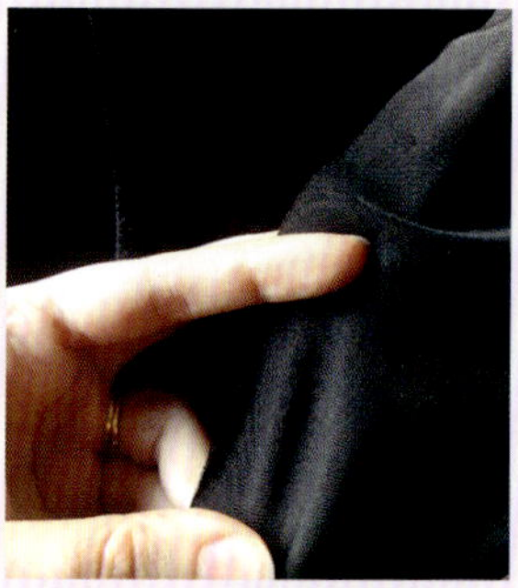

Velour (commonly a knit base, therefore stretchy and more affordable)

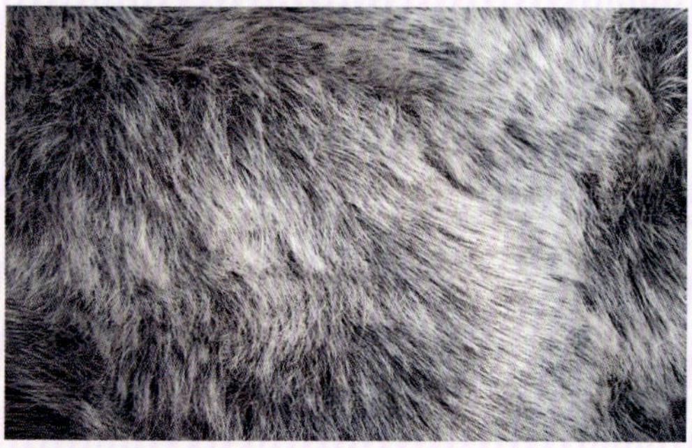

Faux fur

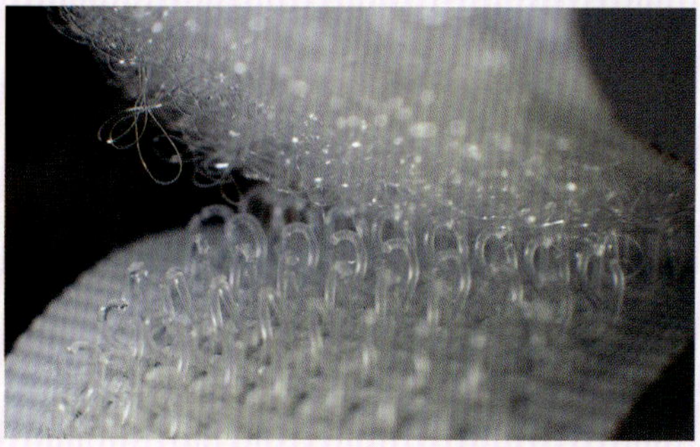

Velcro

Non-woven Fabric

This is a textile where fibers are not interlocked by weaving or knitting, but rather pressed and bound together with heat, solvents, or mechanical/chemical procedures (or a combination of all). Some examples of non-woven fabric common to home sewing are shown here.

Some of these have an additional backing, (as shown: the white layer in the pleather picture) which could be made out of knit or woven fabric. This adds support to the structure of the fabric and comfort to the wearer, since some of these choices can be pretty rough against bare skin. Another characteristic of these textiles is that they won't fray or unravel, but rather can be ripped apart or peeled.

Interfacing, whether it is fusible or not

Film (like vinyl or pleather)

Felt (mostly made of wool)

Leather or fur (directly from animals)

Fiberfill (to stuff comforters, toys, or puff jackets)

CHOOSING FABRIC

Alright, now you know the basic principles of how fabric is made, and that will help you in identifying which fabric is best for each of your sewing projects. While you start developing your sensibility to recognize fabrics, let me share with you my top favorite fabrics to use when sewing and a few more fabric-shopping tips!

THINGS TO KEEP IN MIND WHEN SELECTING FABRICS

I think of these three Ps when fabric shopping to make the best decisions. As you'll come to find, fabric shopping and sewing are sometimes two entirely different hobbies; in order to avoid a fabric stash full of useless materials that don't translate into sewn garments, I try my best to consciously choose my fabrics.

Purpose: What performance do you need from certain fabrics? Why are you choosing one fabric over another? Knowing the purpose of a certain fabric in an specific garment is key to choosing the right textile. For example, when sewing a placemat, ideally we would choose a sturdy, close-woven material contrary to a sheer, slippery, delicate one. We use it to protect the tabletop, so it needs to be thick. It also needs to be easy to clean if something spills, hence why we choose a close-woven textile (it also brings a certain structure to the dining set).

On the other side of the spectrum, for instance, a beach cover-up needs a flowy, sheer, and lightweight fabric. It wouldn't be comfortable to wear a heavy, rigid, denim fabric to the beach, even if the quality of said denim is exceptional!

We need to focus on the purpose of the fabric and how it will interact with the environment it will be put in, to enhance the final product. Aspects to consider when thinking about the purpose of fabric:

- **Drape:** How rigid or flowy does the garment need to be? How difficult will a drapey material be to sew?
- **Weight:** Is it a seasonal garment? Does it need to have a heavier textile to serve a certain purpose?
- **Composition:** I prefer natural fibers, and I bought a heavy-weight, pure linen fabric for a white shirt. Sadly, it rarely gets used because it's prone to wrinkles and a nightmare to iron. This is not to say that synthetic is better than natural; it's just information to factor into your decision when buying fabric for a particular project.
- **Stretch:** Due to fit and construction, some garments simply won't work with a stretchy fabric. Others can't exist without it. Sewing pattern instructions will let you know when to use stretch fabric or not—always follow those indicators to ensure accurately fitting garments.
- **Care:** Some fabrics are hard to care for, like fabrics with embroidery, sequins, fur, or fillings. If you want an easy, everyday top to do chores in, go for a textile that's easy to care for.

Price: There are as many price points as there are fabric styles, and we each have a different sewing budget. With this section, I don't aim to crown one price range as "the correct one"—instead, I suggest you go for less-pricey options as you learn. Practicing on thrifted fabric, discounted cuts, or old clothes can be a great way to optimize your budget while still learning your skills. There is no need to splurge on fabric that is being used for practice.

But what if I am absolutely in love with an expensive fabric?

In my sewing practice, I buy less-expensive fabric to try out new sewing patterns. This provides me with a wearable toile (practice garment) I can use to perfect fit and construction before making the final garment with the more expensive fabric.

Once I am satisfied, I give myself permission to buy a different fabric, maybe a bit more expensive or special. This way I ensure that the splurge will be used in a project I will use again and again. Of course there are also some fabrics that are worth splurging on—for example, the fabric I used for my wedding dress was definitely worth the expenditure!

Other instances could be a high-quality wool or some custom-print fabric. Of course, you can always buy a fabric just because you are absolutely in love with it!

Personal Style: Last but not least, keep in mind your personal style while shopping! When I first started sewing (it occasionally still happens!), I went with sheer, shiny fabrics full of detail, with sequins or high-contrast floral prints. Once I transformed them into garments, they got little to no use in my everyday clothing rotation. I then figured out what my go-to commonly wearable fabric was—mostly solids with lots of stretch; some velvet for fun, and some pops of color, but nothing as extravagant as before.

After seeing so many fabric options at the store or on a website, it can be hard to focus and decide which fabric will actually work as a new wardrobe item. Envision the fabric as the final garment (or even go fabric shopping with a specific idea in mind!). The same applies to colors: I once went shopping and came out with a bunch of earthy tones, only to be disappointed with how those colors looked on me. Bummer!

At the end of the day, we are sewing garments to wear them, so fabric shopping should be as thoughtful as going shopping for off-the-rack clothes. Analyze how the new additions will fit in with your wardrobe before sewing them. This minimizes waste, useless expenses, and energy spent.

FABRIC GLOSSARY

Here's a list of popular textiles used in home sewing:

WOVEN

Lightweight

- Chiffon

  An extremely lightweight textile, created with a plain weave of yarns in S and Z twist, which creates its sheer and flowy distinctive quality. It's usually made of silk or polyester. Ideal for anything with drape, layered dresses, scarves, or light blouses.

- Gauze

  The threads of gauze vary in tension and twist, creating a sparse, breathable, and thin (yet stable) weave. Usually made of cotton. Recently, double gauze is growing in popularity, where two layers of gauze are attached together at regular intervals, creating a puckered look. Ideal for light and fresh baby clothing.

- Organza

  A highly Z-twisted yarn in a plain weave, this fabric is lightweight, translucent, and rigid (structured). Originally made of silk, it is now easy to find in cotton and polyester. Very popular in wedding dresses and nightgowns.

- Satin

  As its name suggests, satin is a textile created with a satin weave, in which a larger section of thread remains unwoven, creating a distinctive sheen on one face and an opaque surface on the other. It has great drape and a smooth touch, perfect for lingerie, nightgowns, and elegant blouses. It can be found made from silk (the highest quality), or nylon or polyester (more affordable options).

- Sateen

  Another satin weave with a silky touch and light sheen surface. It's different from satin based on its fabric content, generally cotton or rayon, making it very durable and less pricey than satin.

- Swiss Dot

  A very lightweight base with heavier, opaque embossed dots woven all-over it. This type of weave is called fil coupé. This fabric is great for delicate dresses or blouses and can be found in traditional cotton or polyester which is a bit more sheer.

Chiffon

Organza

Regular gauze

Double gauze

Polyester satin. Notice the right side of the fabric (closer to the camera) has slightly more sheen and a lighter color than the wrong side of the fabric, which looks more opaque.

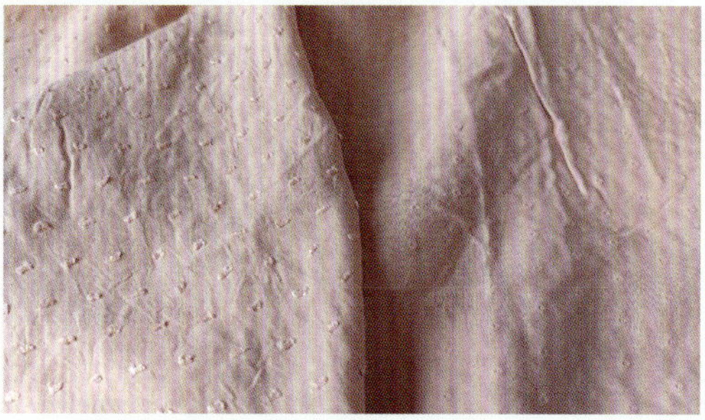

Swiss Dot. The right side of the fabric is pictured on the left side, with the wrong side of the fabric on the right.

Medium Weight

- Muslin

  A true muslin textile has thinner weft threads than those in the warp. Usually made of cotton in a plain weave, ideal for toiles and construction mock-ups.

- Poplin

  A very tightly woven textile, usually made of cotton in a plain weave where the warp has double the thread density than the weft, creating its crisp and durable qualities. Great for structured and light garments like shirts and skirts.

- Taffeta

  A stiff and structured textile created by interlocking threads in a plain weave. Its iridescent quality can be achieved by combining different color threads in both weft and warp, and it is known for its distinctive rustle sound when handled.

- Crepé

  A plain weave with highly twisted threads either on warp or weft, once the textile is off the loom these twisted threads curl, creating its characteristic crinkled look. It can be made from silk, cotton, wool, or synthetic fibers. Has good drape so it can work for dresses or blouses.

- Crepé Back Satin

  Created with a satin weave, this textile offers a different aspect on each side contrary to the traditional crepé. With sheen on one side (satin) and opaque and crinkle on the other (crepé) this fabric can work as structured dresses or light blouses playing with both sides.

- Georgette

  A full crepé, where both warp and weft have highly twisted threads giving its crinkle effect to both sides of the canvas. This textile is sheer and flowy, made in silk, rayon, polyester, or cotton.

- Eyelet

  This textile is created with a plain weave as base and an intricate openwork embroidery, where the pattern leaves holes to see through the fabric. This is a common summer staple for its breathability ideal for light blouses or dresses.

- Shantung/Dupioni

  A plain weave distinctive for its irregular surface due to irregular silk threads. It has a light sheen and slight mechanical stretch. This textile has no drape, but a more stiff and structured quality ideal for sculptural garments like darted dresses, coats, or jackets.

Heavy Weight

- Velvet

  A heavy and warm textile, created with either plain or satin weave as base and a pile weave to achieve that plush and soft surface. Due to its stiff nature it's ideal for tailoring, overcoats, trousers, and home decor.

- Corduroy

  A ribbed pile weave creates the distinctive textured lines for this textile. Ideal for cold-weather garments like trousers, jackets, tailored suits, or home decor.

Muslin

Poplin

Taffeta

Crepé

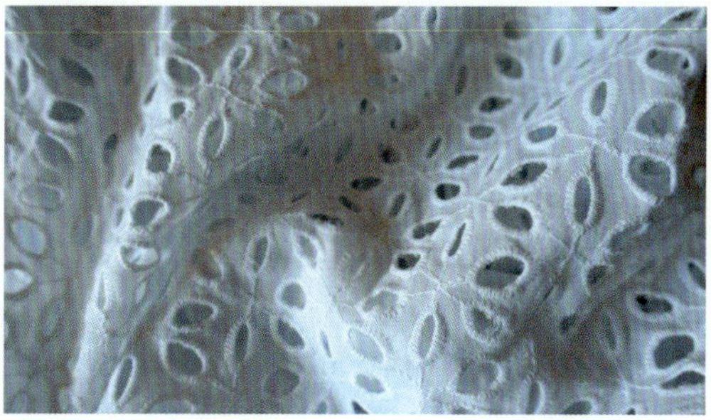

Eyelet

Shantung

Velvet

Corduroy

- Twill

  Created with the weave of the same name, this textile is characterized by diagonal lines through the entire canvas. Found in cotton, wool, or polyester, it is great for suits, trousers, or structured garments for its adaptability, durability, and readily accessible nature.

- Mikado

  A heavy and structured textile with light sheen, traditionally made of silk but now common in polyester, this textile is perfect for sculptural sleeves, dresses, or jumpsuits.

- Denim

  A twill weave with indigo-dyed threads on warp and raw threads on the weft create its characteristic denim blue which gets beautifully discolored with time and use. This textile is durable, strong, dense, and adaptable. Its weight can vary and modern versions include elastane for added stretch.

Woven Pattern Effects

The following fabrics create different visual patterns due to the weave and a combination of thread colors in warp and weft, making these shapes and colors the structure of the fabric canvas itself, contrary to prints which are stamped on top of a plain fabric canvas, where this motifs can be found too.

- Chambray

  A lightweight plain cotton weave with colored threads in warp and white threads on the weft that create a marbled / mottled look. Ideal for shirts, shorts, or bedding.

- Pinstripe

  Traditionally a twill weave with a dark base (black, gray, navy) and white thin lines also known as chalked stripes. Very common for tailored suits, hats, or coats.

- Plaid/Tartan

  A symmetrical crisscross pattern of Scottish origin—typically found in a combination of red, black, white, and green.

- Gingham

  Also known as Vichy in Europe, this pattern consists of only two colors (traditionally red and white or blue and white) creating symmetrical checks varying in tone. In the white and blue example, some squares are purely blue, others purely white, and the rest a light blue due to both colors combined by interlocking together.

- Houndstooth

  Originally from France, this weave is created with only two colors, usually black and white or beige and brown, creating what seems a broken checked pattern. In its smaller scale it's a common textile for traditional menswear but larger scales bring a modern side to it.

- Glen Plaid

  Also known as Prince of Wales, this twill weave is made of wool, usually with two colors (there are variations using up to three). Inside the middle squares we can find a houndstooth effect. This textile is commonly used for tailored garments.

Twill

Mikado

Denim

Chambray

Pinstripe

Plaid

Gingham

Houndstooth

- Argyle

  A diamond shape pattern, where solid colors are overlapped by a dotted line creating other diamond shapes.

- Herringbone

  Defined as a broken twill weave, this textile is woven with two contrasting threads for that "zigzag" effect, usually made of wool. Very common in tailoring, coats, jackets, and suits.

- Jacquard

  This is the generic name of a weave capable of creating intricate and complex designs beyond the checkered or straight variants seen above. Gobelin, damask, lancé, and brocade are some variants of Jacquard fabrics.

- Damask

  A subvariant of Jacquard, this textile is traditionally monochrome, creating the shapes and drawings with different weaves to achieve different sheens and opacities that outline said shapes. Nowadays more colors are added either by weave or print keeping the flower-like shapes characteristic to damask.

KNIT

- Jersey

  A textile with mechanical stretch widthwise due to one single thread being interlocked with itself in a weft knitting machine with one row of needles. On the right side we find a very subtle vertical ribbed pattern whereas on the wrong side a horizontal netting can be perceived. Perfect for tees, underwear and tops.

- Interlock

  Another type of weft knit, only this time it is knitted with two rows of needles, creating two layers of jersey knitted back to back. Both faces of this fabric are the same and it has less stretch.

- Ribbed

  By alternating between knit and purl stitch an effect of raised bands is created. This fabric is specially stretchy widthwise and common in cuffs, neckbands, or hems in sweatshirts, for instance.

- Piqué

  This fabric is best known in polo shirts, it is a knit with alternating stitches that create those tiny mountains and valleys characteristic of polos. It is lightweight and very breathable, perfect for loungewear.

- Spandex

  Also known by its commercial name, Lycra, this fabric is as stretchy as it gets. You will find it blended with other fibers, and it's especially useful for swimwear (due to being chlorine resistant), activewear, lingerie, and sportswear.

- Fleece

  A medium-weight knit fabric with wooly pile weaves on one or both sides, which makes it soft and warm. Usually slightly stretchy widthwise, it is great for sweatshirts, pajamas, or pants.

Glen Plaid

Argyle

Herringbone

Jacquard

Damask

Jersey

Ribbed

Piqué

- Mesh

  A very open and breathable grid usually made of polyester or nylon combined with spandex. It can vary in weight and openness, going from tiny and lightweight for lingerie mesh to bigger and stiffer for shoes, for instance.

- Velour

  A knit fabric with a pile weave similar to velvet, the only difference being the base canvas. Because velour is knitted it also has mechanical stretch, drapes more, and is usually less pricey. It is great for leggings, jumpsuits, tops, or dresses.

SPECIALTY FABRICS

- Quilted

  Created by two or more layers stitched together, usually with a filling between to create a padded surface. The stitching can be simple or very intricate depending on the design. This textile is perfect for winter garments to create insulation, keeping you warm and cozy.

- Flock

  This fabric has a plain base with an additional "print" of texture. Usually this texture pattern is opaque to add a visual contrast to the fabric.

- Tulle

  A loose grid of thin threads that create a translucent textile usually used as base for delicate embroidery. It can be created in layers to give more structure, volume, and resistance.

- Lace

  A very lightweight and translucent fabric, created with a sort of netting base alternating between fills and gaps subsequently enriched with additional designs and patterns. Lace is very popular to embellish nightgowns, lingerie, dresses, or accessories. Combined with elastane it can be used for body-shaping garments.

PRINTS

Unlike fabrics woven specifically to create visual patterns, such as plaid or houndstooth, print fabric relies on an additional step subsequent to weaving to add the visual interest. Print fabric usually has a defined border near the selvedge and the color rarely penetrates to the wrong side of fabric. Prints can be applied to fabric in the following ways:

Block printing: A manual process where the print is engraved into a stamp (this could be a wooden block, linoleum, or sponge) that is pressed into color, then into the fabric to stamp the design.

Screen Printing: The design is transferred onto a screen where everything is covered in a resistant material except the motif, where the color will pass through in order to stamp the fabric. Each color needs a screen, limiting the available screens per design.

Cylinder Printing: A metallic cylinder is engraved with the design (similar to screen printing). The fabric passes between the cylinder and a rolling pin to get printed.

Spandex

Fleece

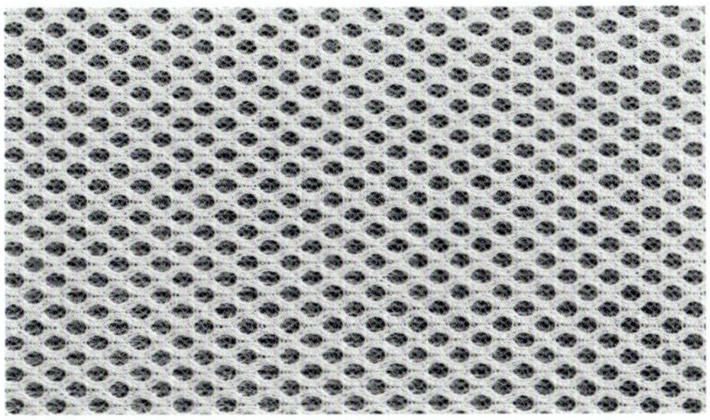

Mesh

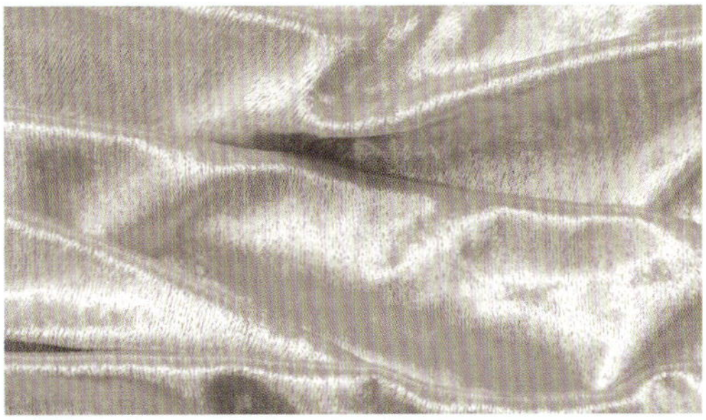

Velour

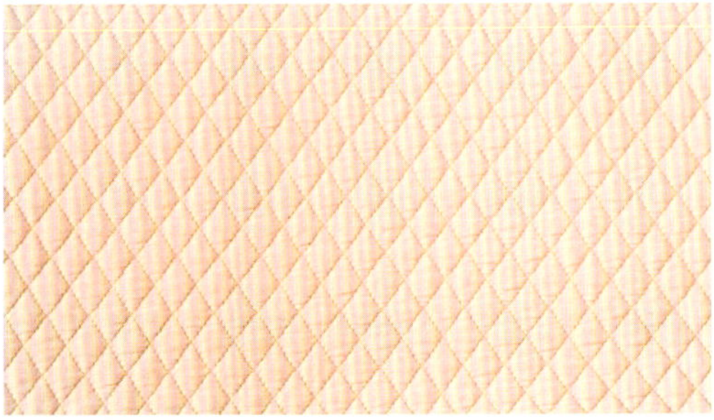

Quilted

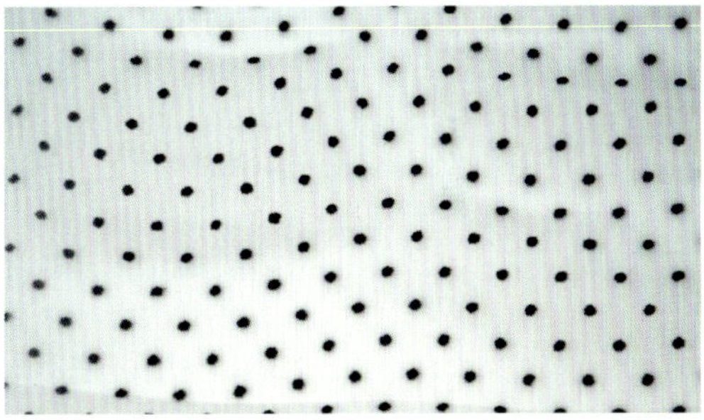

Flock

Tulle

Lace

Digital Printing: The process where an inkjet printer stamps the design onto fabric. This allows for more colors in the design. Prints can have different directions in which to be perceived as "correct," these are:

- **Directionless:** Where the print looks the same whether it's straight or upside down.
- **Directional:** It has a clear right direction, when placed upside down it looks the other way around.
- **Border Print:** The motif is only placed on one border of the fabric.

Some popular print designs are shown on the opposite page.

TRIMS AND NOTIONS GLOSSARY

- **Bias Tape:** A strip of fabric cut on the bias (ergo its name) used to cover the raw edge of fabric to keep it from fraying.
- **Piping:** Similar to bias tape, this trim has an inserted cord to create a filled edge.
- **Elastics:** Varying in width and material, their stretchiness is ideal to create waist-bands, cuffs, or hemlines that gently grip the body.
- **Fusible Bonding Web:** A lightweight tape that works as glue when heated with an iron. Ideal for quick hemline fixes.

Bias Tape

- **Flat Buttons:** Flat shapes with two or four holes that are attached to fabric by thread. This can be done either by hand or sewing machine.
- **Shank Buttons:** These buttons have a loop on the bottom side that can be sewn to the fabric with thread.
- **Fabric Covered Buttons:** These buttons are covered by fabric. They usually attach in the shank button style.
- **Grommets:** Metal rounds used to reinforce a cutout hole in a piece of fabric, such as for shoelaces or cords.
- **Snaps:** Composed of two elements, one piece is pressed inside of the other securing the two sides together. They vary in size and material.

Camouflage

Chevron

Paisley

Polka Dot

Stripes (vertical and horizontal)

Tie Dye

Floral

Ikat

- **Hook & Eye:** This is a metal duo used to subtly fasten garments. Composed of one hook that slides inside the eye, generally made of metal.
- **Zippers:** Used to fasten longer openings in a quick and easy pull. Some are attached at the bottom (such as in trousers), and some are two separate pieces (such as in a leather jacket). They vary in length, color, and material to blend with different projects.

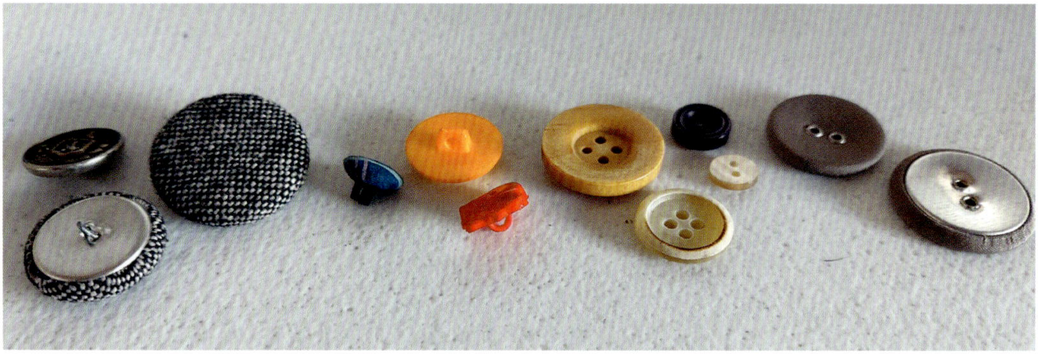

From left to right, metallic engraved shank button, fabric covered buttons, plastic shank buttons, flat buttons with four holes, flat buttons with two holes, flat fabric covered buttons.

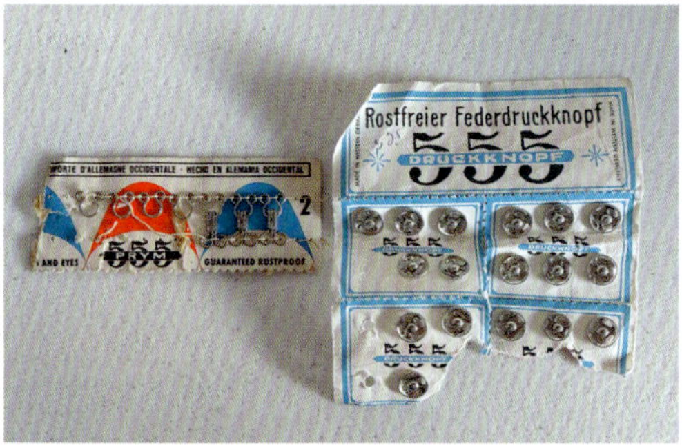

Vintage hook and eye to the left, and metallic snaps to the right.

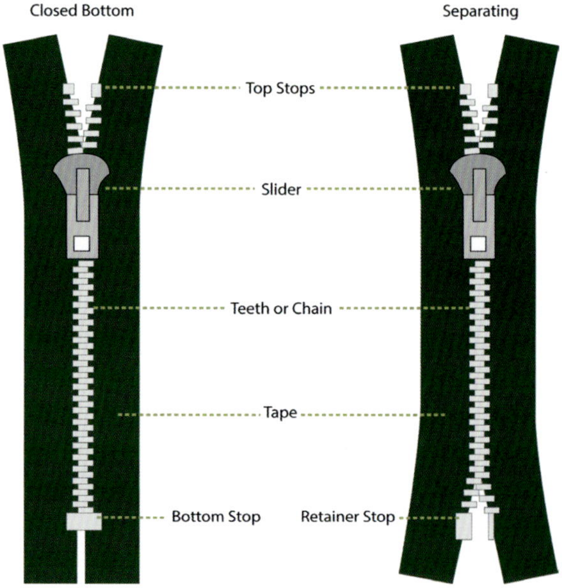

ANATOMY OF A ZIPPER Zippers usually differ by the type of teeth:

- **Nylon Coil:** Flexible, inexpensive, and typically the teeth match the color of the tape. The teeth are visible from the right side of the garment.
- **Invisible Zipper:** This is also a nylon coil but the teeth are only visible from the wrong side of the zipper, while the slider lies on the right side. Typically used for nightgowns to hide the zipper.
- **Metal Chain:** The metal teeth are pressed to the tape, ideal for heavy duty projects like leather, jeans, or bags.
- **Plastic Molded:** The teeth are directly molded onto the tape, and work great for other heavy-duty projects.

Nylon Coil

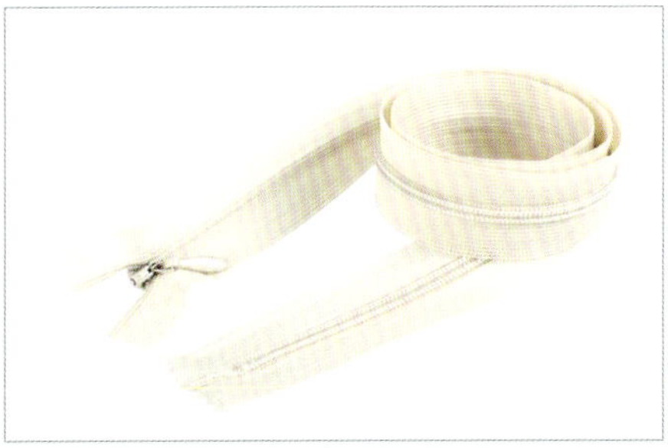

Invisible Zipper

Metal Chain

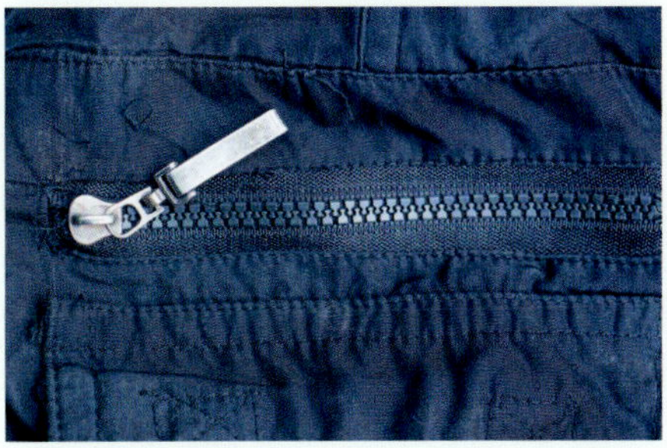

Plastic Molded

CA02776
Polyester
274 yds/vgs

CHAPTER 2

Tools and Equipment

In this chapter I'll show you the common tools used for sewing. We'll dive into the beginner must-haves, the advanced options, and the nice-to-haves.

While it is tempting to picture ourselves in a brand-new sewing room with the latest sewing gear, remember it is easier (and more affordable) to start small and build up. Furthermore, you'll discover your particular way of working with the tools. Some nice-to-haves may be essential to you once you try them, whereas some sworn must-haves in the sewing community could be unnecessary to you.

TRACING

For a novice sewist, a few tracing and drafting tools are needed (even if you're not drafting your very own patterns from scratch just yet). You'll want to be able to re-trace the pattern and to transfer the information on the pattern pieces to the fabric. I'm sure you already have most of these tools lying around.

BEGINNER

- **Pencil:** I prefer to use a harder graphite pencil like H/2H. I find that the softer the pencil, the easier it is to smudge the final traced pattern piece.
- **Eraser:** I usually go for the squared ones—the straight edges make erasing easier.
- **Tape Measure:** You'll use the soft plastic type, not the metallic retractable one. Make sure it has centimeters on one side and inches on the other. You'll find sewing patterns with centimeters and inches, so it is better to be prepared for both.
- **Ruler:** A plastic school ruler works great, best if it is 30 cm long for longer lines.
- **Tracing Paper:** I always use tracing paper or white tissue paper (the kind you can wrap gifts with). It is affordable, easily found, and has the right weight and transparency.

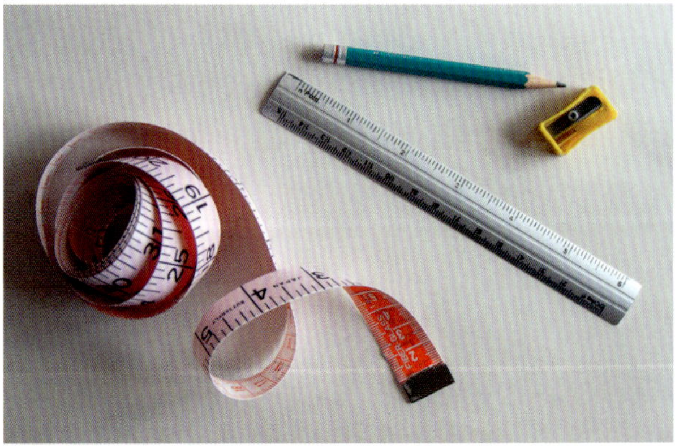

ADVANCED

- **French Curve:** Comes in handy when tracing armholes and necklines, or curvier darts, for instance.
- **Square Ruler/Carpenter L:** Great for tracing longer lines, especially when drafting your own patterns because most starting lines need to have a perfect 90° angle.
- **Tailor's Chalk:** Instead of a pencil, you can trace pattern pieces or notches with tailor's chalk. It is machine-washable so it leaves no trace on the finished garment; but it also fades easily while you're working so I don't consider it too beginner friendly.
- **Paper:** If you are ready to do a few modifications on existing patterns or drafting your own, a common A4/Letter sheet won't be too useful. Look for rolls of paper to draft that are 24–28 inches wide.
- **Tape:** I love Scotch magic tape. It is light on tissue paper and won't rip it. Useful when joining together two pattern pieces to adjust or cut.

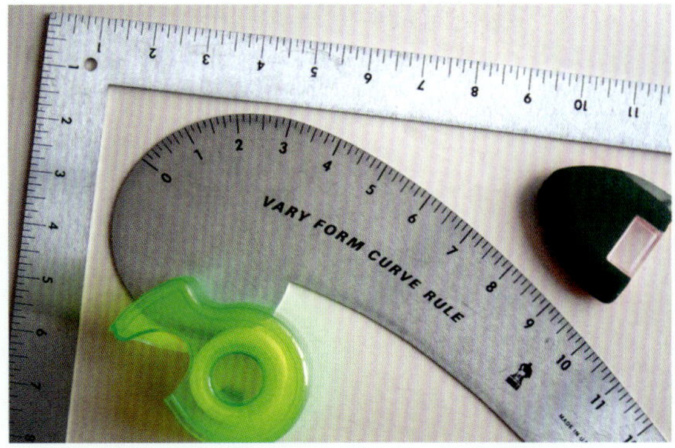

From left to right: A square ruler, tape, French curve, and tailor's chalk

From top to bottom: A quilting ruler, tracing wheel, and carbon paper

NICE-TO-HAVES

- **Quilting Ruler:** If you can afford the extra expense, a quilting ruler is worth every cent. Its transparency makes tracing every line a breeze. I use it to add seam allowances and lines on the garment for pressing, and for drafting.
- **Tracing Wheel:** Marks a line of tiny dots on paper or fabric without leaving a color trace, unlike a pencil or tailor's chalk. Useful to transfer pattern pieces onto fabric when used with dressmaker's carbon paper.
- **Dressmaker's Carbon Paper:** A sheet of paper that comes in different colors to mark lines onto fabric when pressed with the tracing wheel. It is washable and can be reused multiple times.
- **Kraft Paper:** If you wish to cut the same pattern pieces over and over again, I suggest you create templates out of a heavier weight paper for durability.

CUTTING

Cutting seems pretty straightforward. You just need scissors, right? Well...

When sewing, the very least I use is three cutting tools—one for fabric, one for paper, and one for threads. I'll further explain in the Beginner section below, but I've found that cutting is the part of the process where sewists differ the most. My tip is to play around until you find a method that suits you best, and you might use less (or more) than my three must-have cutting tools.

BEGINNER

- **Fabric Scissors:** Commonly referred to as fabric shears, these scissors are larger and heavier than regular scissors. It is of the utmost importance to never cut anything that isn't fabric with them. If you do, they'll lose their sharpness, and that could damage your fabric while cutting.
- **Paper Scissors:** Any kind of scissors will do. Use them to cut paper pattern pieces only. If you don't, you jeopardize their sharpness.
- **Clippers:** Clippers are ideal for cutting threads, which you'll do *all the time.* But, you could easily replace them with your preferred tiny scissors. Just make sure you have something to cut smaller things aside from your main fabric shears.
- **Sewing Pins:** You don't cut with these, but they are essential when cutting pattern pieces from fabric with shears. The pins attach the pattern to the fabric securing it in place so the shears can cut out the garment pieces accurately.

The fabric scissors are the largest. The clippers are the smallest.

ADVANCED

- **Rotary Cutter:** Imagine a pizza cutter for fabric. This is my preferred method to cut out the fabric of smaller pattern pieces and skip the entire sewing pin attachment. Instead, you just secure the paper pattern pieces with pattern weights. I only use it for fabric—never paper! Like with fabric shears, cutting materials other than fabric will dull the blade.
- **Cutting Mat:** When using the rotary cutter, you must use a cutting mat, otherwise the surface where you are cutting will be cut too (or at least damaged). My mat is 12–18 inches because I only use it for smaller pieces, but bigger ones are also available.
- **Pattern Weights:** Used instead of sewing pins to secure the paper pattern pieces to the fabric. My tip is to use whatever you have lying around, like heavy candles, soap dishes or your phone. If you are feeling fancy, you can sew your own pattern weights or buy specialty ones.

NICE-TO-HAVES

- **Cutting Table:** Commonly found in industry spaces or with sewists who have room for a large table. The traditional way of cutting fabric is by moving around it, keeping it still so you don't risk shifting the pieces. While this is perfectly achievable on the floor, a cutting table at home would be really nice to have.
- **Pinking Shears:** These are the zig-zag-bladed scissors. They are commonly suggested to finish fabric edges because they prevent fabric from fraying. In my experience, they are great for quilting and patchwork projects but not so much as an alternative for finishing garments.
- **Duckbill Scissors:** Also known as appliqué scissors, these are handy when removing excess fabric from a seam. The higher blade prevents the fabric you don't want to trim from peeking over.

Pattern weights and a rotary cutter on top of a cutting mat

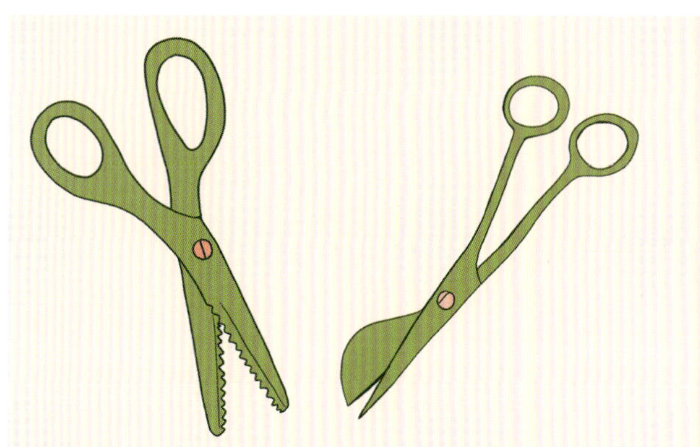

Pinking shears (left) and duckbill scissors (right)

SEWING

Some tools already described, like sewing pins or clippers, are also used in the sewing part of the process. But there are some others that are particular to this step that I'll cover in depth below. You'll also notice I go from beginner to nice-to-haves, because I feel you can upgrade and get advanced with the same set of beginner tools.

BEGINNER

- **Sewing Machine:** The "must-have" stitches are straight and zigzag. Ideally, if you can afford the expense, look for one with a buttonhole option and a stitch width adjustment button. The latter gives you tons of room to work with different stitching needs, like topstitching and understitching, for instance. Usually, sewing machines come with a needle and bobbin.
- **Sewing Machine Needles:** These are specific to sewing machines, different from the hand-sewing variety. They come in different sizes for different uses, which I'll detail ahead.
- **Thread:** The ultimate beginner-friendly thread is polyester, and the two must-have colors are black and white. You'll start growing your color collection as you go.
- **Sewing Pins:** As described before, pins are essential for attaching pieces of fabric together to construct the garment. They prevent any shifting while sewing.
- **Iron:** Pressing is essential to high-quality garments. Don't skip on having one, even if it's very basic.

- **Seam Ripper:** Your best friend when mistakes arise. This tool unpicks stitches easily.
- **Hand-Sewing Needles:** Some projects will require you to hand sew, so make sure to have a couple of hand-sewing needles with you at all times.
- **Extra Bobbins:** Bobbins are the plastic or metallic rounds where the bottom thread of the machine is set. Having four or five to begin with is useful when changing thread color.

NICE-TO-HAVES

- **Sewing Gauge:** A 6-inch ruler commonly used to measure smaller distances like buttonholes or to achieve even hemlines, for instance.
- **Sewing Clips:** Used for heavier weaves, thick seams (like in quilting), or leather garments (which you can't pierce with sewing pins because the tiny hole won't ever disappear). These are for very specific projects, so your beginner toolkit will be complete without them.
- **Bobbin Box Organizer:** A handy place to store all your existing bobbins.
- **Tailor's Ham:** A curved cushion to work as an iron surface to press curved seams like darts, collars, or sleeves.

UNDERSTANDING YOUR SEWING MACHINE

You just got your first sewing machine, whether it is brand new or a family heirloom, and you are sitting in front of it already creating a thousand outfits in your head. BUT (insert record scratch here) how are you supposed to know how to operate such a thing?

If you have your sewing machine's manual with you this will be much easier. If not, don't worry because the basics are generally the same amongst most sewing machines. I'll guide you through the basic components of a sewing machine and its accessories, such as needles, bobbins, and walking feet, so you can start sewing with more confidence in no time.

SEWING MACHINE

This wonderful tool creates continuous stitches to join two or more pieces of fabric together. A stitch is created by two separate threads that interlock together, one coming from the top of the machine, and the other from the bottom—with the fabric placed between the two.

Machine Components that Correspond to the Top Thread

Thread Spool Pin: This is where the journey of our thread starts, where the thread will spin as the machine starts stitching (**FIGURE 2.1**).

Thread Guide: A disc that holds the thread for it to pivot toward the take up (**FIGURE 2.2**).

Thread Take Up: A lever that moves up and down along the needle as the sewing machine is stitching (**FIGURE 2.3**).

Needle Bar: This connects the thread take up to the actual sewing needle. The needle is secured to it by a screw. This screw can loosen or tighten its grip for the purpose of changing needles (**FIGURE 2.4**).

Needle: The essential component that makes the top thread at the spool interact and interlock with the bottom thread at the bobbin (**FIGURE 2.5**). More about needles and their sizes in the next section.

TIP Commonly, this entire thread journey is properly signaled with arrows on the machine. The top thread tension can be adjusted with the wheel tension control.

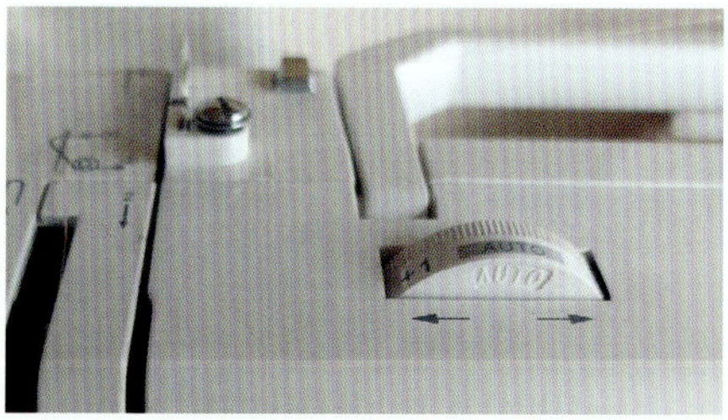

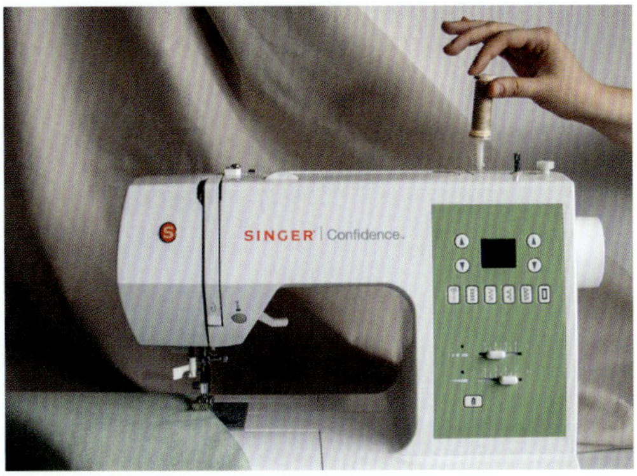

FIGURE 2.1

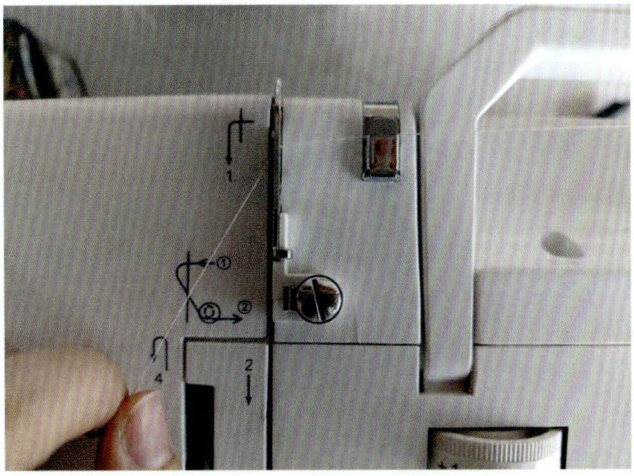

FIGURE 2.2

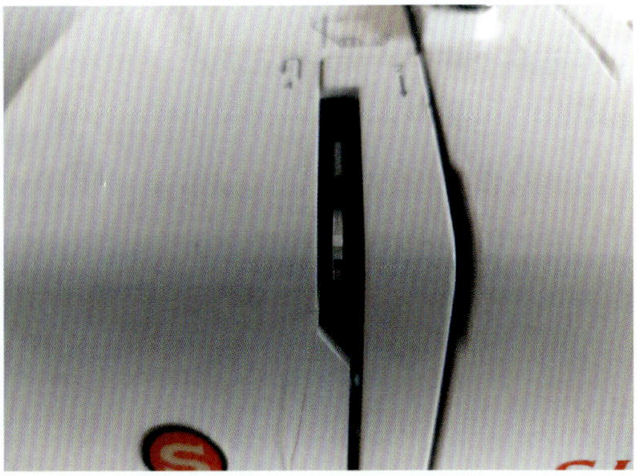

FIGURE 2.3

FIGURE 2.4

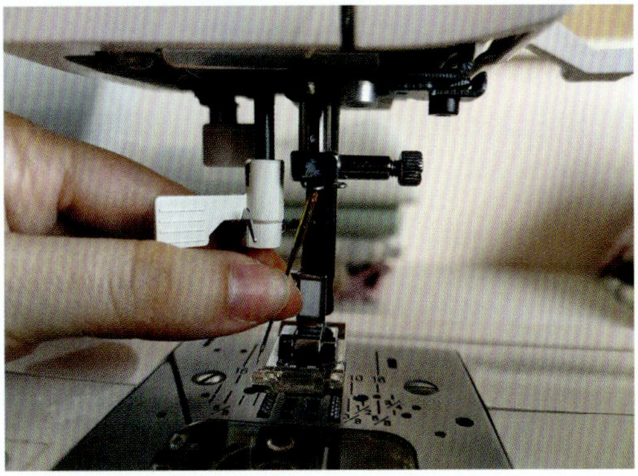

FIGURE 2.5

Machine Components that Correspond to the Bottom Thread

While the top thread comes from a spool, the bottom thread comes from a bobbin, which must be wound by the sewist. Bobbins can be plastic or metal depending on the sewing machine.

Bobbin and Bobbin Slot: The place where the thread-filled bobbin is inserted **(FIGURE 2.6)**.

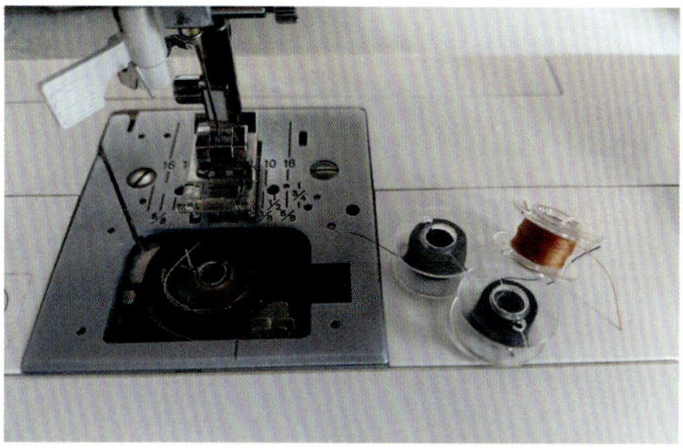

FIGURE 2.6

Bobbin Winder Shaft: This shaft spins as you press the foot controller to wind the thread to the bobbin (**FIGURE 2.7**).

Bobbin Winder Stop: This prevents the bobbin from over-filling (the white knob to the right of the bobbin) (**FIGURE 2.7**).

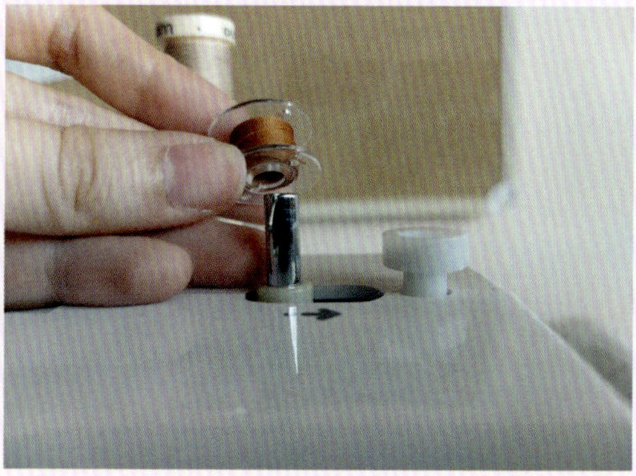

FIGURE 2.7 *The winder shaft is the metallic piece to the left, and the stopper is the white plastic piece to the right.*

Machine Components at the Needle Plate

Presser Foot: This holds the fabric in place against the feed dogs. There are different feet for different uses. The ones I mostly use are (from left to right) the quilting foot, the zipper foot, the buttonhole foot, and the walking foot (**FIGURE 2.8**).

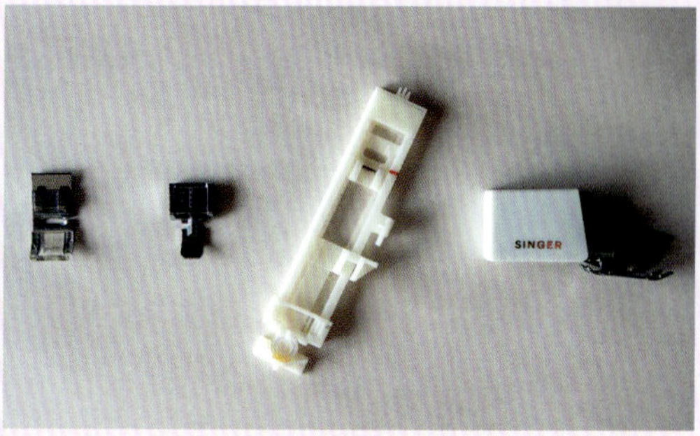

FIGURE 2.8

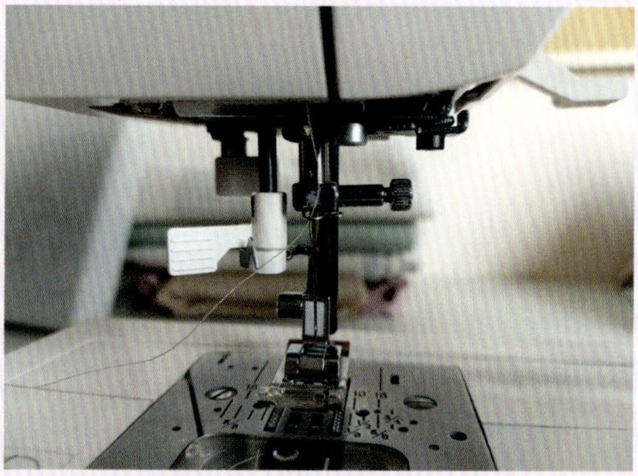

FIGURE 2.9 *The presser foot (the metallic piece below the needle) attached to its place.*

Feed Dogs: These are teeth-like lines at the needle plate (below the presser foot) that pull fabric to the back with each stitch (**FIGURE 2.10**). They move in sync with the speed of the needle. This is what makes the fabric move through the machine without you needing to pull it.

Presser Foot Lifter: A lever that moves the foot presser up to release the fabric or down to secure it (**FIGURE 2.11A–C**).

Foot Release Button: Pressing this releases the attached foot so it can be changed for another (**FIGURE 2.12**).

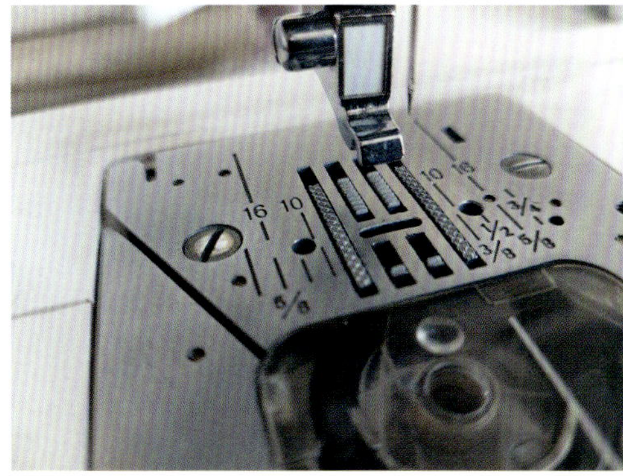

FIGURE 2.10

FIGURE 2.11A *Presser foot lever, all the way up*

FIGURE 2.11B *Presser foot lever, halfway down*

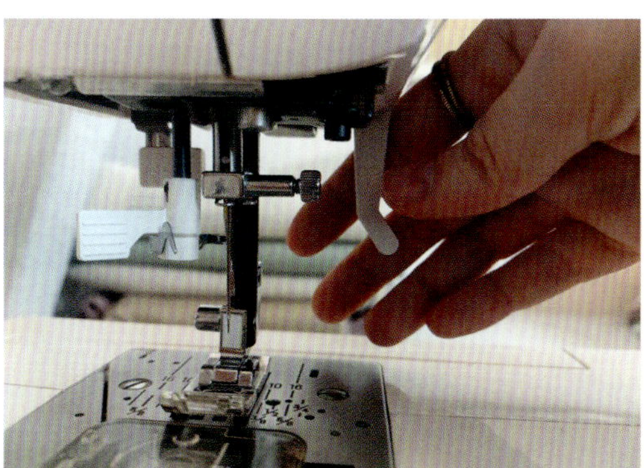

FIGURE 2.11C *Presser foot lever, all the way down*

FIGURE 2.12 *Foot release button*

Inner Components: Depending on the machine, the inner components could be different—but this is the inside of mine once the needle plate is removed (**FIGURE 2.13**). The bobbin slot is removable for easier cleaning (**FIGURE 2.14**).

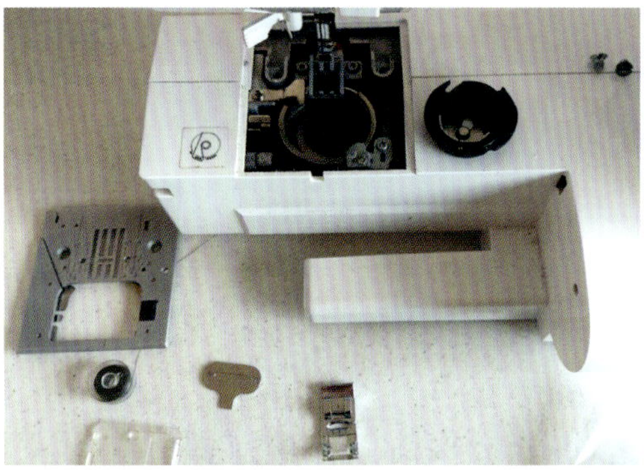

FIGURE 2.13

FIGURE 2.14

Machine Components to Create Stitches

Foot Control: Stepping on this control starts the action of sewing (**FIGURE 2.15**). How fast the needle will stitch is dependent on how hard it's pressed.

Hand Wheel: This gives you manual control of the needle (**FIGURE 2.16**) and is usually to the right side of the machine. If turned toward you it will stitch, and if turned away from you it will go in reverse.

Reverse Stitch/Back Tack: When pressed, this button creates a double passing of stitches to secure the beginning or end of a seam (**FIGURE 2.17**). I've had other machines where it's not a button but a lever to pull down.

This is the perfect time to explore your sewing machine. Find each of the components mentioned above, get familiar with your machine's manual, try threading it, and get her ready for the sewing exercises we'll start in chapter 5.

FIGURE 2.15

FIGURE 2.16

FIGURE 2.17 *Reverse stitch/back tack button*

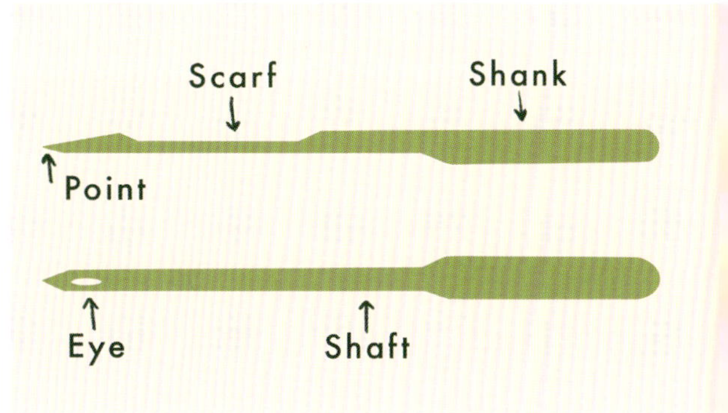

SEWING MACHINE NEEDLES

As we discussed in the previous section, stitches are created by top and bottom threads interlocking with the essential help of the needle. Sewing needles vary in sizes and uses, but they all share the same parts:

Shank: The upper part of the needle, it has one flat side and one rounded side so you can identify how to insert the needle into the machine. The flat side goes to the back (it also has the size and type of needle engraved here).

Shaft: Refers to the length of the needle, from the end of the shank to the very pointy end. The thicker the shaft, the bigger the needle number. That's why for lightweight fabric you need a lower needle number, so it punctures through with a slimmer shaft.

Eye: The hole where you insert the thread.

Point: The end of the needle. The shape may be different depending on the needle type and its purpose.

NEEDLE SIZE

When purchasing or trying to figure out which needle size you have in your hands, you'll see two different numbers followed by letters.

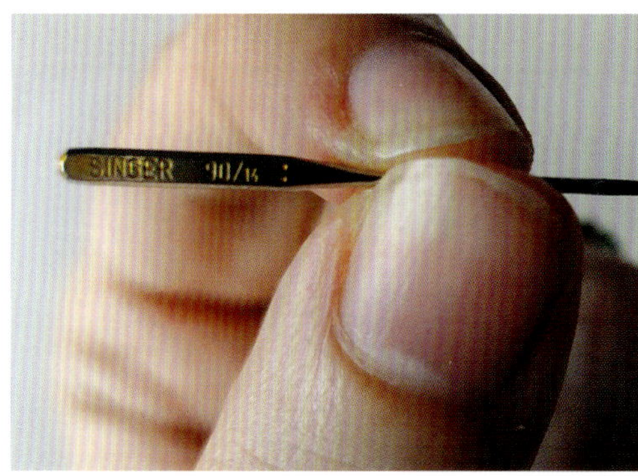

The numbers represent the thickness of the shaft. The larger numbers on the left come from the European sizing system, and the smaller numbers are from the North American system. The smaller the number on the needle, the lighter the fabric it can sew; the larger the number, the heavier the fabric it can pierce.

EUROPEAN NEEDLE SIZE	NORTH AMERICAN NEEDLE SIZE
60	8
65	9
70	10
75	11
80	12
90	14
100	16
110	18
120	19

As for the letters, here's a chart with the abbreviations you'll see most frequently as a home sewist, what they mean, and which fabric you can use them with.

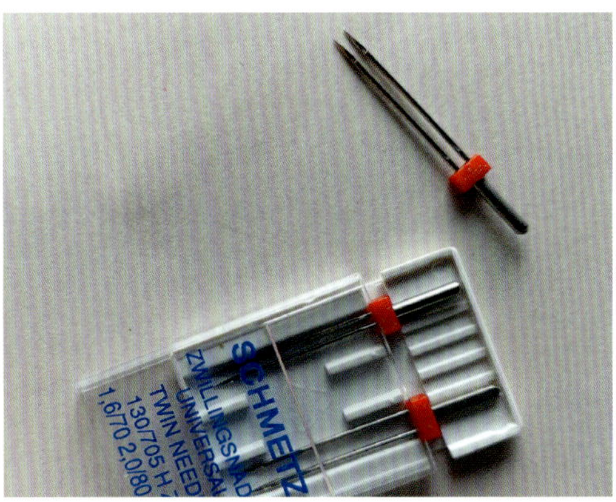

A twin needle shank.

NAME ABBREVIATION	USE
Universal H	The go-to needle for any project. It's multipurpose and will work with most fabrics perfectly.
Ballpoint H-SUK	The best needle to work with stretchy fabric. It has a rounded point to take care of your knit and not pierce it to the point of breaking it. Ideal for jersey knit fabric.
Stretch HS	For very stretchy knits, it has a medium ballpoint to pierce without pulling the fabric. Would work great with elastic lace for lingerie.
Sharp/ Microfiber HM	A very sharp needle perfect to puncture through fabric with high thread count, such as satin.
Jeans HJ	A very sharp and sturdy needle meant to pierce through thick fabric.
Twin needle ZWI	This is a double needle with two different eyes connected to the same shank. Works with a regular sewing machine to create a coverstitch.

TIP It is key to get familiar with needle types, sizes, and their uses. You'd be surprised how frequently a messy, ripped, or torn seam is just the result of a wrong needle in use. In my experience, the combo of thread tension, needle size, and stitch length is the make-it or break-it for a project.

TIP Before sewing your actual project, try a few stitches with different settings on a scrap of the fabric you are using. You are looking for a neat result of even stitches. Play around with the variations. Maybe the needle size is on point, but the thread has too much tension, so adjust accordingly. Or maybe the issue lies with the type of stitch. The more you try new settings, the faster you'll get a natural sense of what works.

HOW TO CARE FOR YOUR EQUIPMENT

Here are my top five tips for taking care of your tools:

1. Never use your scissors interchangeably!

   Remember, long-lasting sharp blades are the result of keeping their tasks separate. Have one pair for fabric and one pair for paper (at least) at all times.

2. Remove all sewing pins!

   I cannot stress this one enough. While at the machine, remove all pins before they reach the sewing needle. You don't want them to collide because it can cause severe damage to your machine.

3. Keep all instruction manuals!

   Most issues I've encountered with my machines have been easily solved with the corresponding manual—this saves tons of time in searching for the right answer.

4. Clean your machine!

   Too many times I have ruined a seam because a huge lump of fluff, fuzz, and thread jammed the bobbin. Save yourself the heartache and clean your machine regularly (this applies to all of your tools).

5. Try to follow best practices!

   Have I been in such a hurry to iron that I pressed directly onto my table without an ironing board? Absolutely! But this is how tools get damaged and ruined. Try your best to take care of your tools at all times, not just when they are falling to pieces.

CHAPTER 3

Sewing Basics: Terminology

In this chapter I'll walk you through one of two main skills that gave me a hard time as I was first starting to sew: The first is learning all of the sewing definitions. Maybe it is the fact that my native language is Spanish, but at the very beginning, following sewing instructions in English proved to be very challenging. Aside from learning how to sew, I had to learn a whole new set of words for this skill. The following is a sewing jargon list with definitions and pictures for you to reference every time you need to. Here I'll expand on frequently used words and terms in garment construction.

SEWING JARGON

Back Tack: Also known as reverse stitch, a back tack is an additional two or three backward stitches at the beginning and end of a seam to secure the stitches from unraveling.

To see this in action, visit the video gallery at rockynook.com/sewing_videos.

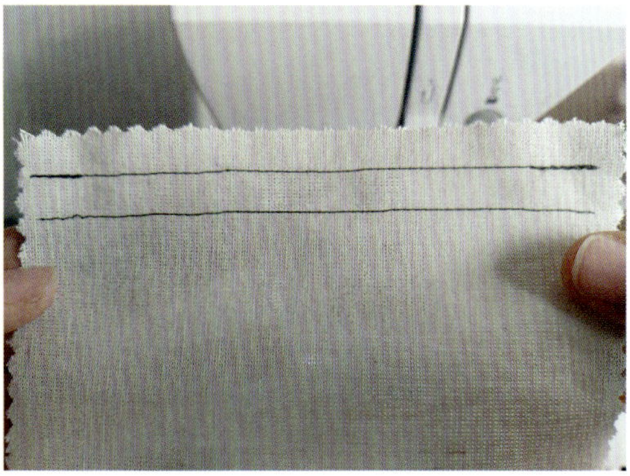

The top line of stitches has back tacking on each end, the bottom line of stitches does not.

Basting Stitch: This is a longer length stitch used to temporary hold fabric together. It is longer to make the "unstitching" easier and faster.

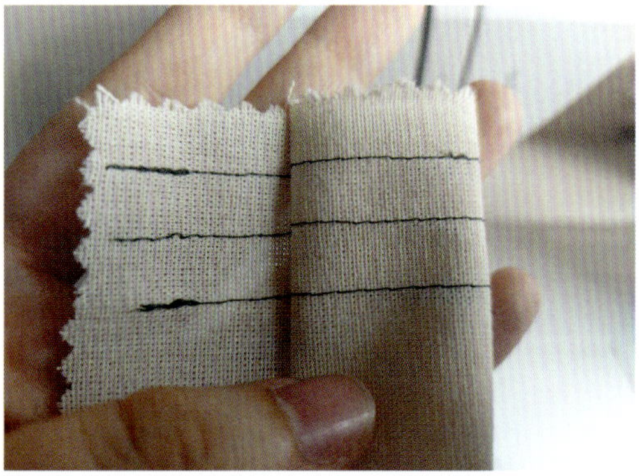

Three lines of stitching: standard stitches with back tack (top); standard stitches without back tack (middle); basting stitches (bottom)

Bias Cut: This refers to placing and cutting the sewing patterns onto fabric at a 45° angle from the selvedge. This gives more drape and a little bit of give to the fabric.

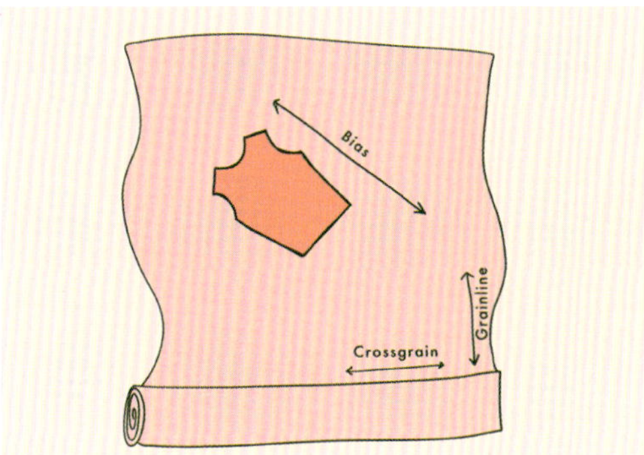

Center Front/Center Back: This is the axis right in the middle of the pattern piece (whether it is bodice or bottom).

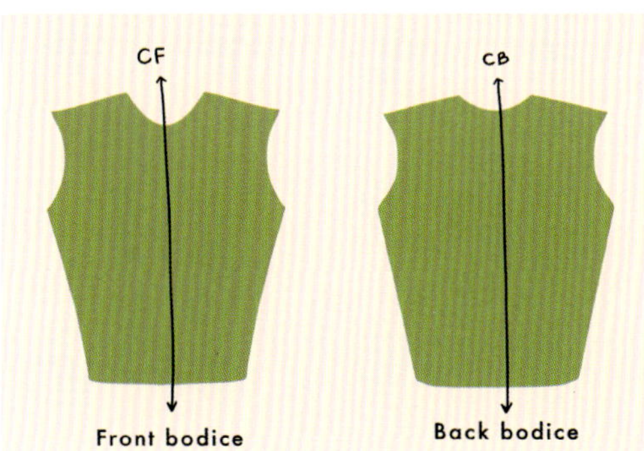

Clip: Doing small cuts to the fabric. I do it regularly on the seam allowances of curved seams to help the fabric lay flat and crisp.

Contrasting Thread: Using a thread color that stands out against the fabric.

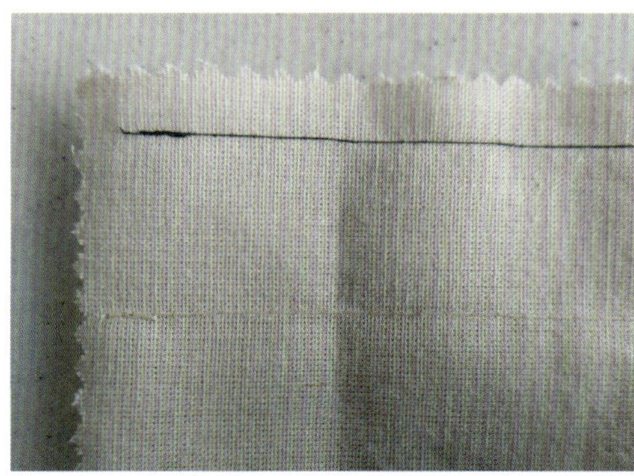

A dark green thread vs. a light, off-white thread below

Crossgrain: Placing and cutting the sewing patterns onto fabric in a perpendicular position from the selvedge.

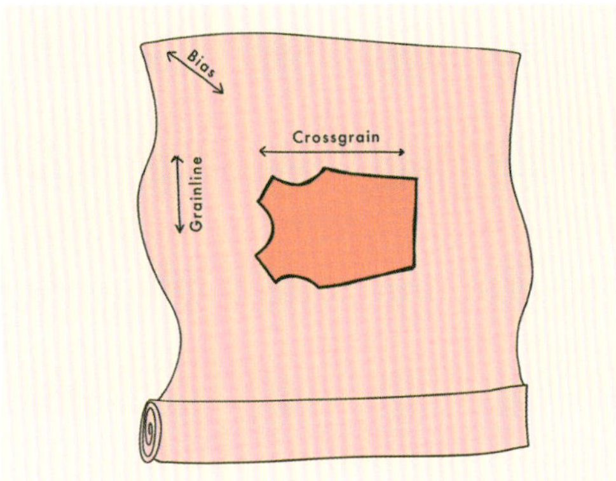

Cut on Fold: Fold the fabric matching wrong sides together, ensuring the pattern piece fits on top of the folded side. Match the arrows in the pattern piece with the folded edge of the fabric, then cut. This yields a symmetric mirrored piece in one cut.

Placing your pattern piece to be cut on the fold

Darts: An area (usually the shape of a wedge in the pattern) that is stitched together to create volume and help shape the garment to the body.

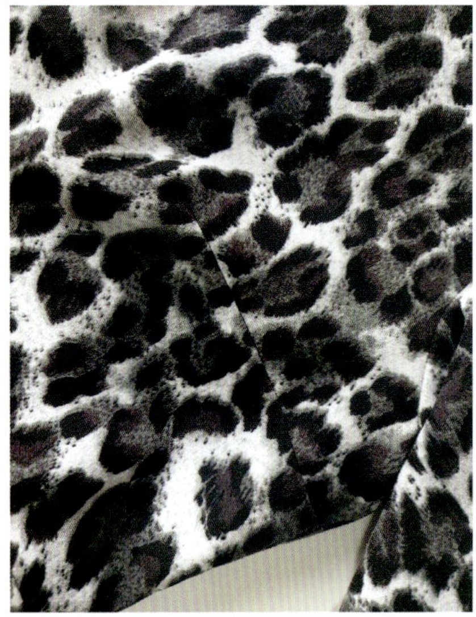

A dart, from the outside of the garment

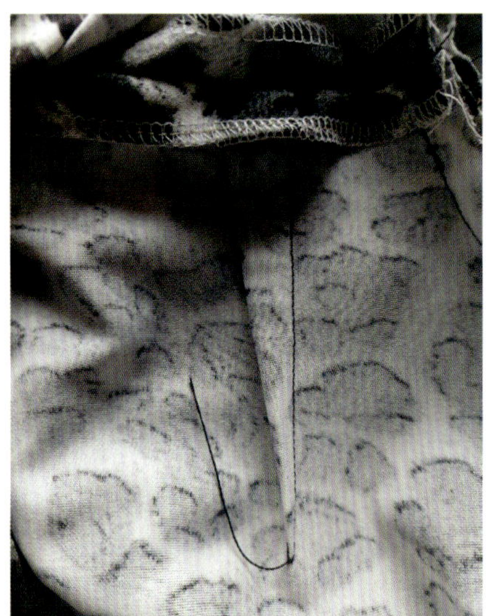

A dart, from the inside of the garment

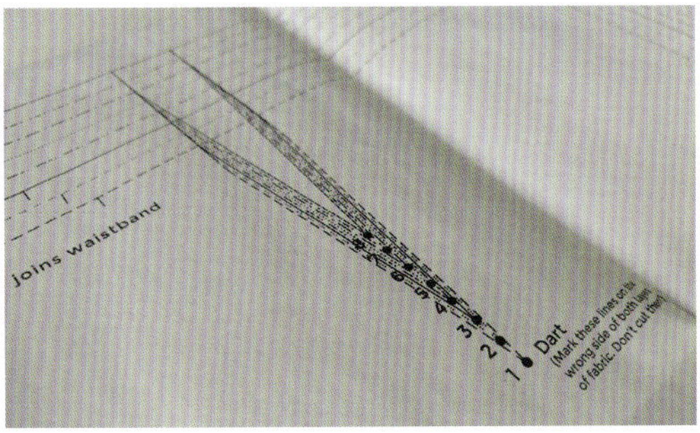

A dart indicator on a pattern

Dots: A symbol in pattern making that signals where to match different pattern pieces if they don't line up directly at the edge of the pattern.

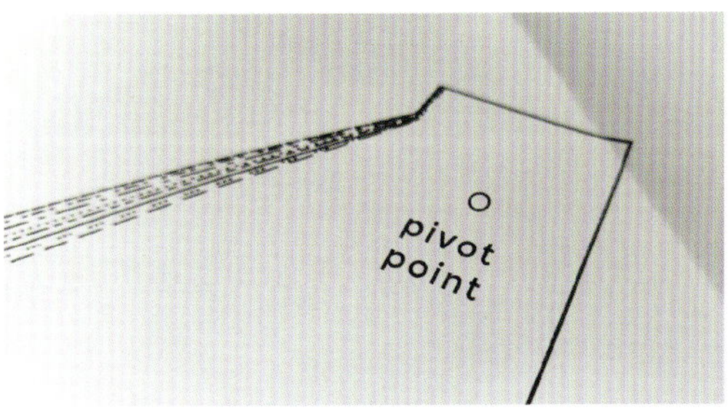

Facings: A narrow layer of fabric that faces the inside of the garment. It is used to finish the raw edges of the garment, enclosing them hidden inside.

Finger Press: A pre-step to ironing by simply pushing down the seams with your fingers.

Finish: The last treatment to any raw edge. The most common version is using the overlock machine. This prevents the fabric from unraveling and keeps the garment neat.

Fabric finished with overlock

French Seams: A type of seam that encloses the raw edge with two passes of stitches. The first one is done at ¼ inch from the raw edge with wrong sides together, then the seam allowance is trimmed down to ⅛ inch. The second pass is done with right sides together at ⅜ inch to complete a ⅝-inch seam allowance, for instance. In case of a smaller allowance, the width needs to be adjusted. This step-by-step process is detailed for the Tote Bag project in chapter 6 (see page 112).

Grade: Cutting down the seam allowances in a staggered way to reduce bulk.

Grainline: Placing and cutting the sewing patterns onto fabric parallel to the selvedge.

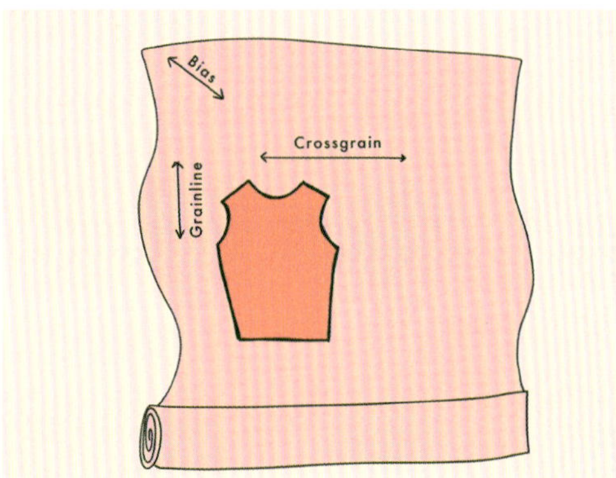

Interfacing: An additional layer of fabric (can be woven or knit and can vary in weight—my favorite is the fusible type) used to stabilize the main fabric.

Lining: Fabric used inside of the garment to add opacity to a lightweight, transparent fabric or to add structure and resistance.

Main Fabric: Also known as "self," this refers to the fabric you'll show on the outside of the garment.

Matching Thread: Using a thread color that blends with the fabric.

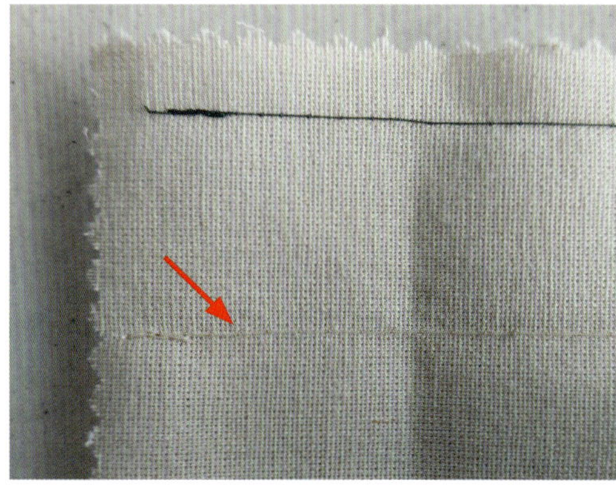

Muslin: Also known as toile, a muslin is a first attempt at constructing a garment using a cheaper fabric with similar drape and feel to the final fabric. This practice mock-up ensures the fit and design are correct.

Notches: A symbol in pattern making on the edge of the pattern piece. Notches signal where to match different pattern pieces together. A single notch is used for all front pieces, and double notches are used to identify all back pieces.

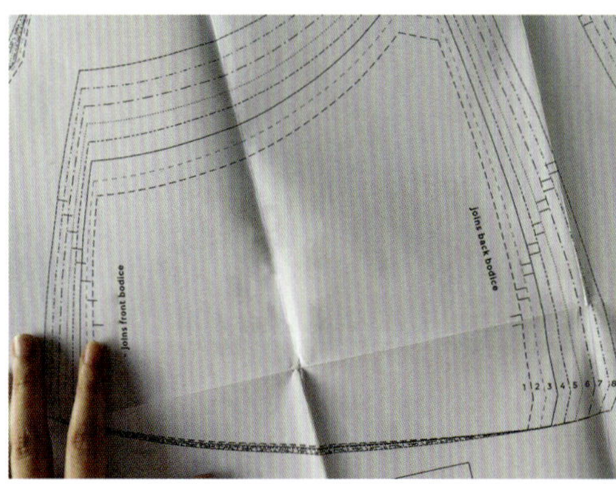

Dress forms with coat (left) and blazer (right) toiles.

Press: Flattening the seam allowances with an iron so the heat keeps them in place.

Press Open: Flatten the seam allowances to either side with the iron.

Press to the Side (Front or Back): Flatten both seam allowances to the same side of the garment, most commonly toward the back.

Right Side: Refers to the side of the fabric you want to have on the outside of your garment, visible to the world. When using a print, the right side is usually brighter in color and more defined.

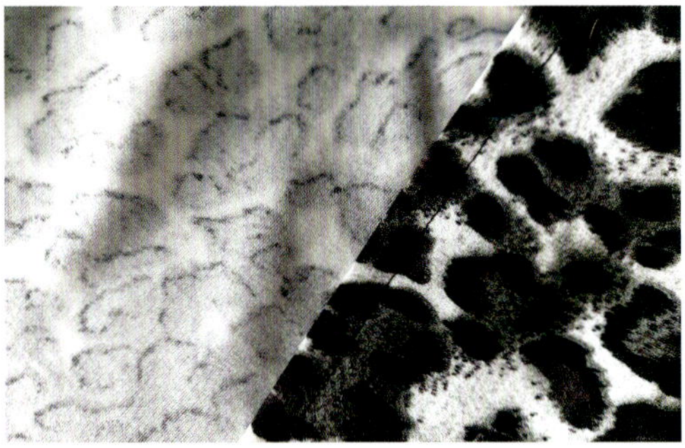

Right Side Facing Up: Directs you how to place your fabric onto your working station for a certain construction step. In this case, with the right side of the fabric facing toward you.

Right Sides Together: Join two pieces of fabric together by making their right sides touch. This way, the seam allowances remain hidden on the inside of the garment.

Seam: A line of stitches that join two materials together.

Seam Allowance: The extra space between the raw edge of the fabric and the seam. Without seam allowances we would be sewing on the very edge of the fabric, which would lead to open seams. Being familiar with seam allowances is being familiar with inches and their fractions. The ones commonly used in home sewing are:

- ⅛ inch: Common: width to trim when sewing French seams.
- ¼ inch: Common for lingerie sewing or stay stitch (temporary stitch).
- ⅜ inch: Frequently used in home sewing patterns.
- ½ inch
- ⅝ inch: Overall seam allowance for specialty seams like French seams or flat-felled seams.
- ¾ inch
- 1 inch

Staystitch: An additional row of stitches, closer to the raw edge of the pattern piece to help certain areas of the garment maintain their shape, usually collars and necklines.

Stitch in the Ditch: A row of stitches landing right in the middle of an existing seam, disappearing from sight (see page 108).

Topstitch: An additional stitch, visible from the right side of the garment that adds strength to a seam—or can simply be decorative!

Transfer: Refers to copying all pattern indicators onto the wrong side of the fabric (see page 74).

Trim: Cutting the seam allowances to half their width (or shorter, if possible) to reduce bulk.

To see this in action, visit the video gallery at rockynook.com/sewing_videos.

Understitch: An additional row of stitches to attach the seam allowance to the wrong side of the garment or facing. This allows the facing to fit perfectly on the inside of the garment and not peek out to the right side.

Wrong Side: This refers to the side of the fabric you want to have on the inside of the garment, hidden from the world. When the fabric has a print or certain texture, usually the wrong side is paler, less clear, or dull.

Wrong Sides Together: Join two pieces of fabric together by making their wrong sides touch.

leg seam
2
3
4
5
6
7
8
FAIRGATE
BY STAMP INC.

CHAPTER 4

Sewing Basics: Making a Pattern

In this chapter I'll walk you through the other skill that gave me a hard time when I was first starting to sew: Using a sewing pattern to make a garment!

Here I'll explain in full detail how the pattern-making process works: how you can use a pattern to turn fabric into a garment you can sew at your own home.

Pattern making and sewing are two different sets of skills: You certainly don't need to know how to draft a pattern to sew impeccable garments, but you'll find that with each project you sew, you'll get more familiar with patterns. In understanding how to read patterns, you make headway toward making your own pattern adjustments and modifications. Knowing the entire process (at least in theory) will give you a fuller understanding of garment making.

PATTERN ANATOMY

First off, what is a sewing pattern?

A sewing pattern is the illustrated roadmap to garment construction. Patterns are templates made of paper or cardbord that is placed onto fabric and indicates how the fabric needs to be cut in order to be assembled into a garment. This template guides us in how to cut the outer silhouette and how to mark the rest of the construction indicators, such as notches, darts, buttonholes, or pleats (just to name a few). These marks aren't necessarily always by the outer edge of the pattern.

How are sewing patterns created?

Sewing patterns are drafted starting from a base block template (also called a sloper).

A sloper is based on specific measurements. In the industry, garment sizes are based on an average of measurements chosen by the brand; when you make a garment at home for personal use, you use the custom measurements of the wearer. A sloper has no wiggle room, no seam allowances, and no style modifications. It is not intended to be sewn or worn, it is just the base drawing. Simply put, it represents the length and width of a certain body from which to design the style.

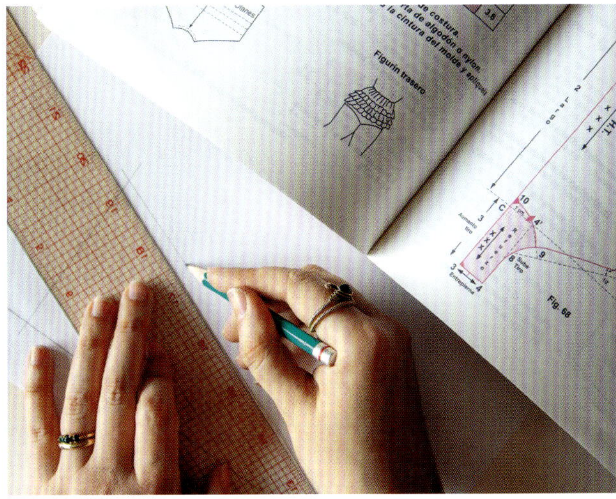

The three basic slopers are:

a. Bodice (**FIGURE 4.1**): Upper torso, from neck to waist. One for the front and another for the back.

b. Skirt (**FIGURE 4.2**): Lower body, from waist to knees (typically). One for the front and another for the back. It can also be transformed into a pants sloper if the lines reach down to the ankle.

c. Sleeve (**FIGURE 4.3**): You only need one for both arms. It includes the front and back view.

FIGURE 4.1

FIGURE 4.2

FIGURE 4.3

HOW TO TAKE ACCURATE MEASUREMENTS

Whether you are drafting your own sloper or simply trying to figure out which size to choose from a pre-existing sewing pattern, taking your measurements accurately is a foundational skill. Accurate measurements help you avoid ill-fitting garments and overworking yourself trying to fix inconsistencies in shapes and measures. It's worth noting that not all slopers or sewing patterns require you to take the measurements of your entire body. For instance, when making trousers, the measurements of your wrist or shoulder are not relevant.

Body measurements are typically taken from top to bottom while standing and are divided between horizontal measurements (widthwise: anything that contours the circumference of the body) and vertical measurements (lengthwise). You'll find that certain measurements require help from a third party, (like the back width), but this usually happens when drafting slopers. In the home-sewing experience, the main measurements you'll need are bust, waist, and hips—which can be easily taken by yourself.

TIP My top tip to accurately take measurements is to follow these steps (this is my best sewing practice!).

1. Stand in front of a mirror, wearing simple clothes. (Avoid anything bulky. Leggings and a tank top work great!)
2. While standing up straight, wrap the tape measure around your body. It needs to be firm against your body but not overly tight.
3. With the help of the mirror, make sure the tape is perfectly parallel to the floor; avoid any tilting.
4. Close your eyes and take a deep breath in and out. (This is where the magic happens!) This restores you to your true self. Oftentimes, we modify our natural pose when being measured, sucking in the tummy, elongating our back, shifting the position of our shoulders—all that could modify the measurements, resulting in an inaccurate sizing and fit. Just relax and be yourself—no one's watching!
5. Take note of the measurement from the tape on a separate piece of paper. I don't recommend you try to remember all the numbers.

HORIZONTAL MEASUREMENTS (FIGURE 4.4):

- **Neck (1):** Measure around the neck, closer to where the shoulders start.
- **Back Width (2):** Measure the distance between the shoulder joints at the back.
- **High Bust (3):** Around the chest, under the arms but above the bust. This measurement tilts a little at the back and that's correct.
- **Bust (4):** Parallel to the floor, taken around the chest at the most prominent part of the bust. (Some suggest this is the nipple, but I've found that's not always the case.)

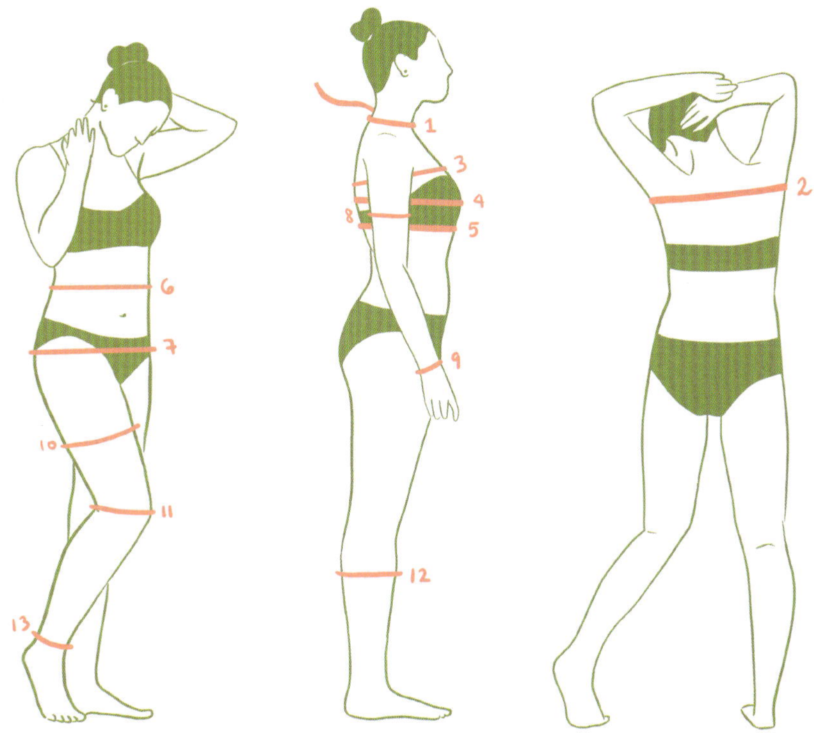

FIGURE 4.4

- **Underbust (5):** Usually needed for lingerie sewing, this is taken around the ribcage right where the underwire of a bra would lay.
- **Waist (6):** Simply think of your waist and instantly rest your hands there. I always use this exercise, because some suggest the waist is the narrowest point of your torso and that's not always the case for everybody. But, we can always tell instinctively where our waist is.
- **Hips (7):** Taken at the hip joint, minding the most prominent part of the buttocks and hips.
- **Arm (8):** Taken around the middle of the arm (humerus).
- **Wrist (9):** By resting the tape on top of the tiny, rounded wrist bone, measure the circumference.
- **Thigh (10):** Measure the circumference around the middle of your thigh (femur).
- **Knee (11):** Measure around the kneecap.
- **Calf (12):** Measure the circumference around the most prominent point of the calf muscle.
- **Ankle (13):** Measure the circumference slightly above the prominent bone at the ankle.

VERTICAL MEASUREMENTS (FIGURE 4.5):

- **Back (1):** Also known as nape to waist, this is taken from the base of the neck to the natural waist. The base of the neck can be taken slightly toward the shoulder, right where the neck starts tilting to become the shoulder.
- **Front (2):** From the same nape-to-waist spot at the back, only this time at the front and the tape measure passes over the most prominent point of the bust.
- **Arm (3):** With the arm slightly folded, this measurement starts at the shoulder joint and ends at the wrist. You can also take note of the elbow measurement here.
- **Hip (4):** Taken at the side, from the waist to the hip joint.
- **Knee (5):** Starting from the natural waist to the kneecap in a straight vertical line.
- **Outseam (6):** The distance between the natural waist toward the floor or the ankle (depending on the design), taken from the side.
- **Inseam (7):** The distance between the crotch and the floor or the ankle (depending on the design).
- **Crotch Depth (8):** While sitting, this measurement is the distance between the natural waist and the seat; taken from the side.

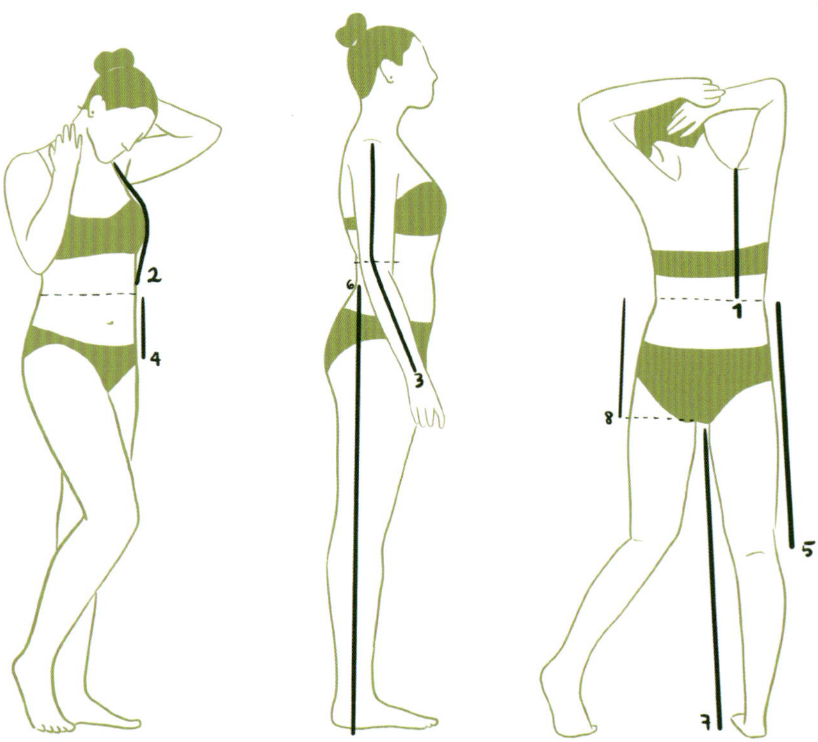

FIGURE 4.5

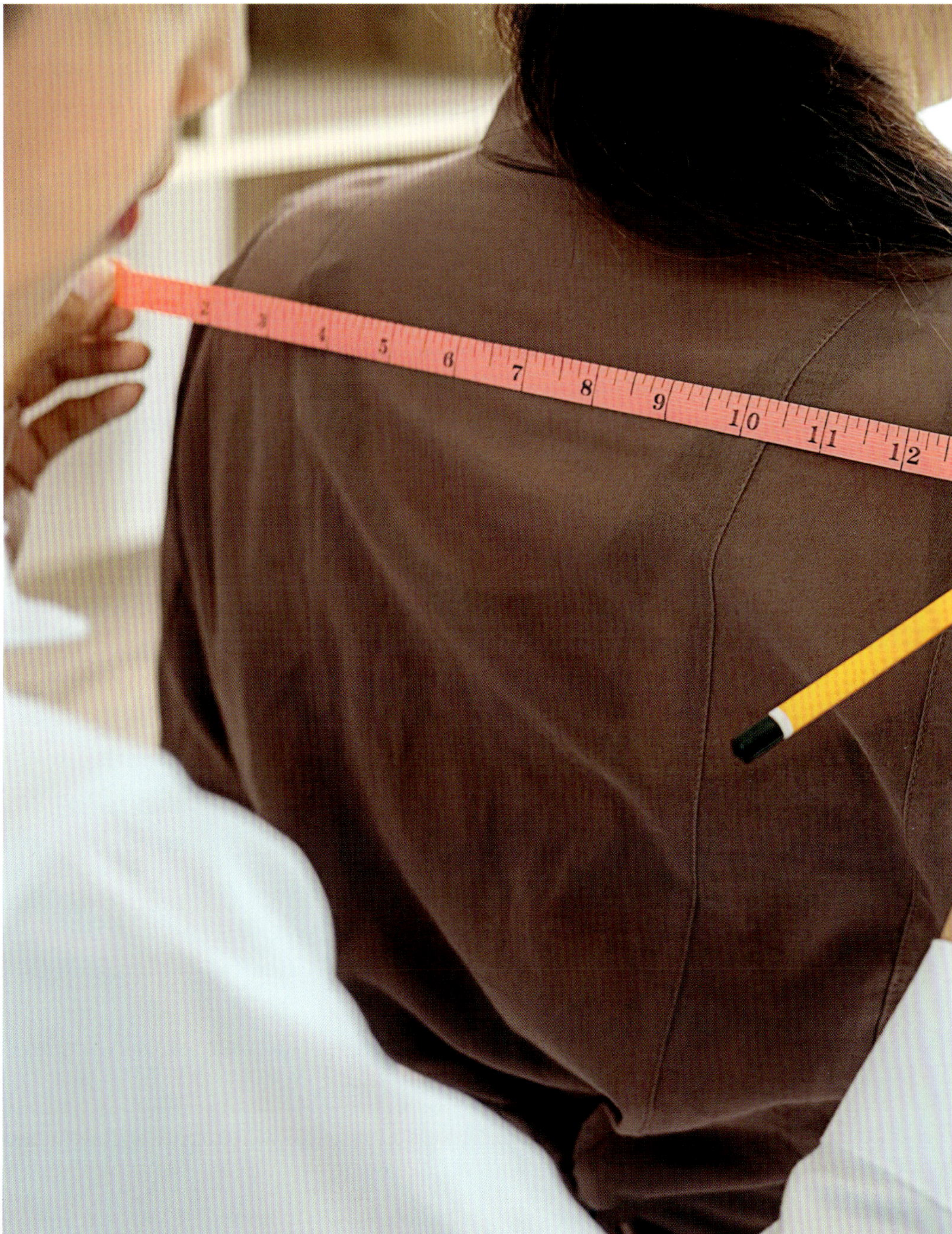
2 3 4 5 6 7 8 9 10 11 12

How is a sloper transformed into a pattern?

By doing length and width modifications to the sloper in certain areas, adding seam allowances and wiggle room (ease), a new style is born (**FIGURE 4.6**).

How can a sewing pattern be transferred onto fabric pieces?

- Attach it directly onto the fabric with sewing pins.

  This is common in home sewing patterns, because the paper is thin and can be easily pierced by pins. Cut the pattern piece out, pin it to the fabric, and cut around the pattern piece. Cut accurately along the edge of the sewing pattern to create the required fabric piece.

TIP You can leave the pattern piece attached to the fabric to keep track of the pieces before sewing (a great trick for novice sewists). This method can't be used with cardboard patterns—they are too thick.

FIGURE 4.6 *With minor modifications from the original sloper, the bottom transformation in light green removes length, adds volume with wedges, and creates a bubble sleeve.*

- Overlay the pattern pieces onto fabric and secure them with pattern weights.

  Using pattern weights is another popular method amongst the home sewing community for securing pattern pieces to fabric. Of course, you need extra equipment other than scissors and pins, such as rotary cutter and cutting mat. Cut as you do in the pinning method, close to the edge of the pattern directly with a rotary cutter. You can also trace the pattern onto the fabric with tailor's chalk, remove the pattern pieces, and proceed to cut the fabric pieces along the chalk lines.

TIP This method is perfect for cardboard patterns, which are too thick to pin to the fabric. In this method, you need to either label your fabric pieces or identify them by shape so you don't lose track of which piece is which once the cardboard is separate from the fabric.

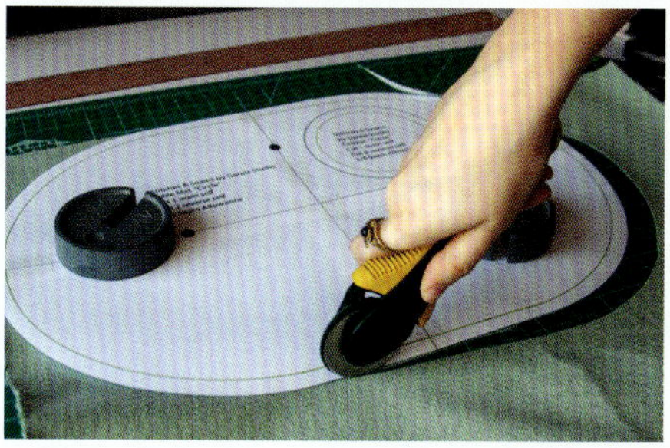

- Use a tracing wheel and carbon paper.

  By placing carbon paper between your fabric and your sewing pattern, you can transfer the pattern markings onto the fabric with the tracing wheel (**FIGURE 4.7**). The tracing wheel presses the color of the carbon paper onto the fabric, leaving tiny dots indicating where to cut.

To see this in action, visit the video gallery at rockynook.com/sewing_videos.

FIGURE 4.7

TIP Purchase a digital PDF sewing pattern, and you'll typically get three files:

1. The instruction booklet for sewing
2. An A0 file to print the pattern pieces with a plotter machine
3. A long PDF file with A4/Letter pages you need to print and assemble to create the whole pattern pieces

TOP TIP: Retracing

My go-to method for long-lasting sewing patterns is *retracing*.

Every time I buy a new pattern, whether it is digital or physical, the paper pattern becomes a valuable possession to me. Let me explain.

When you buy an already-printed sewing pattern, it's the only copy you've got. Cutting out one of the several offered sizes means losing the rest of the sizes for good. Instead, I retrace all the pieces with tissue paper, so I keep the original pattern intact in case I need other sizing options.

In the case of digital patterns, which need to be printed out, the same concept applies. I could cut directly onto my size but that means I would need to print it all over again next time, which is costly (and assembling the home print patterns, sheet by sheet, is a full-time job in itself!).

Take the extra time for retracing. Your future self will thank you!

PATTERN INDICATORS

The following are the frequently used indicators I've encountered in many years of home sewing. Not all patterns have all of them (for example, not all pattern pieces are cut on fold, nor do all designs have pleats). This is a collection of indicators you'll surely use sometime in your sewing journey.

- Cutting line (dotted on multisize patterns) (**FIGURE 4.8**)
- Lengthen or shorten here

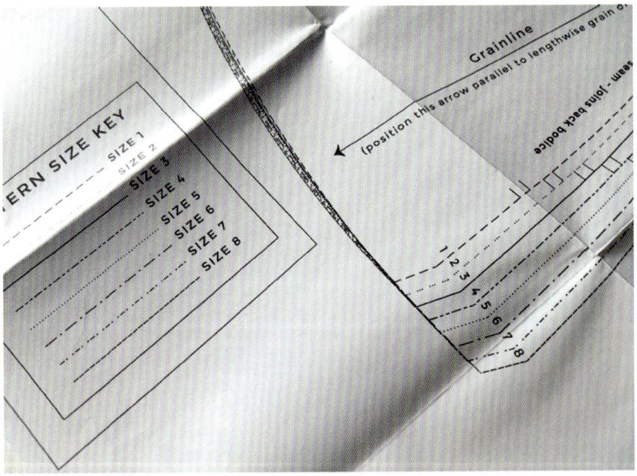

FIGURE 4.8 *Cutting line*

- Cut on fold (**FIGURE 4.9**)
- Grainline (**FIGURE 4.10**)
- Notches (double notch on back) to match seams and to indicate hip, knee, waist, or hemlines (**FIGURE 4.11**)
- Darts (**FIGURE 4.12**)
- Pleats direction (**FIGURE 4.13**)

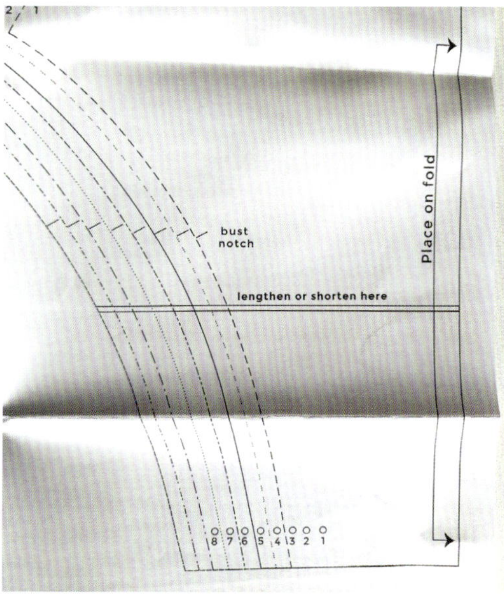

FIGURE 4.9 *Cut on fold*

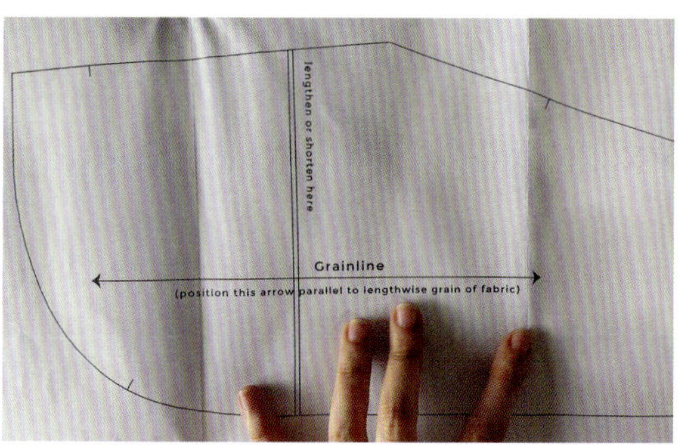

FIGURE 4.10 *Grainline*

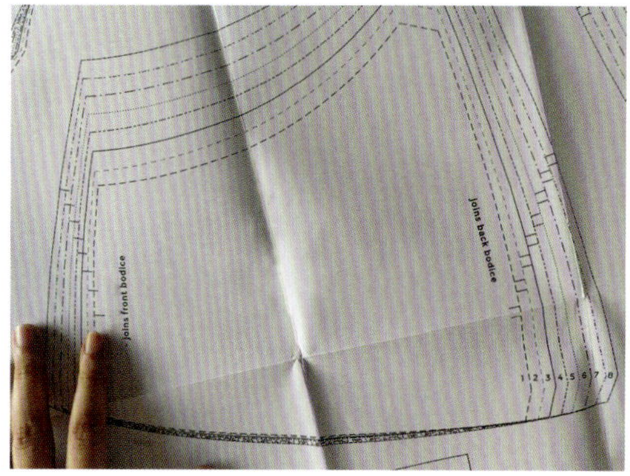

FIGURE 4.11 *Notches*

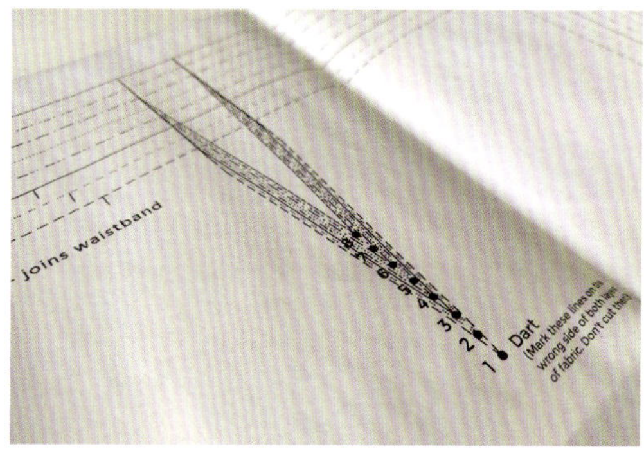

FIGURE 4.12 *Darts*

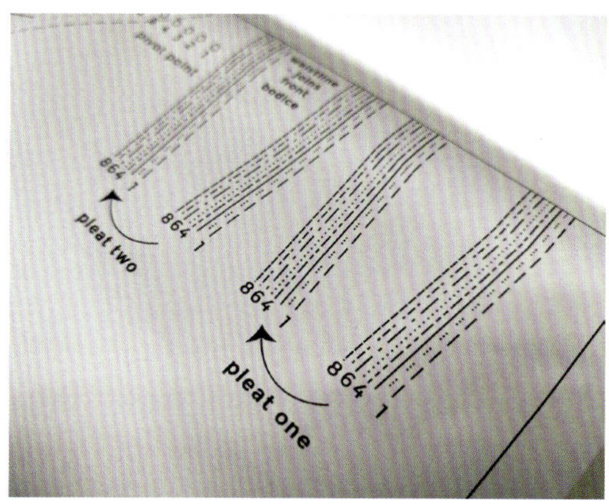

FIGURE 4.13 *Pleats direction*

- Bias (**FIGURE 4.14**)
- Dots (**FIGURE 4.15**)

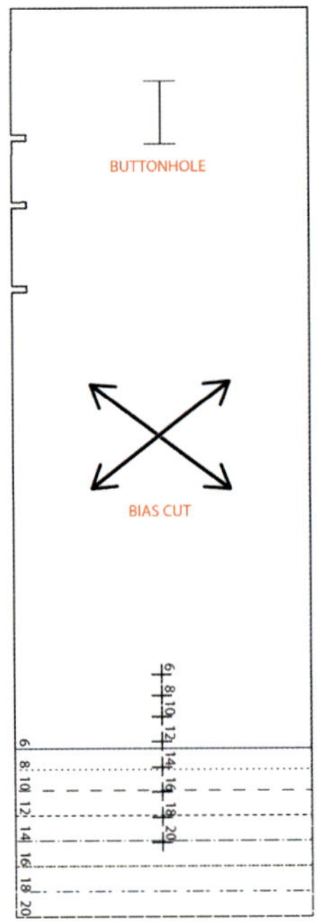

FIGURE 4.14 *Bias*

> **TIP** Don't forget to include the instructions with your retraced pattern pieces!

FIGURE 4.15 *Dots*

PATTERN INFORMATION

All sewing patterns include clear and precise instructional information to achieve a correct assembly of the garment.

EXAMPLE (FIGURE 4.16)

- Brand: Garala Studio Patterns
- Name/style: Ampersand Undies
- Size: Size 12
- Piece name/number: No. 2 Top Back Lining
- How to cut: Cut on fold
- How many pieces: Cut 1 self, cut 1 lining
- Seam Allowance: ⅝ inch

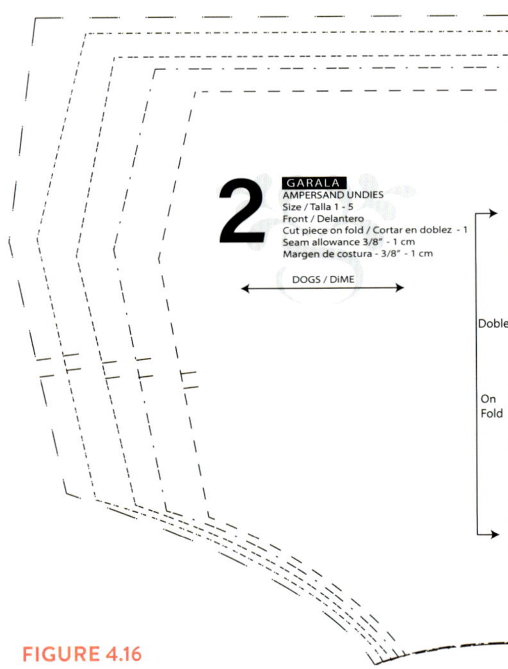

FIGURE 4.16

FIGURE 4.17A

PATTERN PREP WORK

All sewing patterns for this book are available to instantly download at rockynook.com/sewing_patterns.

Printing

There are two pattern formats to choose from:

1. Choose A4/Letter to print at home and then tape together to assemble.
2. Choose Copyshop to print with a plotter machine and skip the assembling (**FIGURE 4.17A**).

Once you have the PDF pattern downloaded into your computer, you are ready to print.

In both formats, you'll find squares measuring 2x2 inches and 3x3 centimeters (in the A4/Letter format you'll find it on the first or second page of the PDF document). This is your verifying tool for scale.

Before printing the entire document, print the page with the square and measure it with a ruler (**FIGURE 4.17B**). If the sizing is correct you are ready to print.

Make sure the printing settings are at 100% scale.

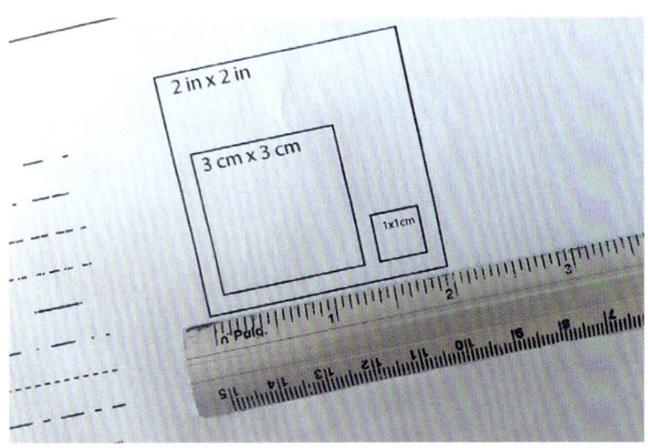

FIGURE 4.17B

Assembling

In the case of printing at home with the A4/Letter format, do the following:

Step 1: Find the illustration with the numbered sequence next to the scale square and place your paper sheets following that drawing (**FIGURE 4.17C**).

Step 2: Using your paper scissors, cut *only* one edge of a sheet, and match it with its neighboring edge. Match the black circles for a precise union and tape the sheets together (**FIGURE 4.18A–E**).

Do the same with the remaining sheets. It is not necessary to cut all edges, as you'll see—you need a lip to rest the neighboring sheet on.

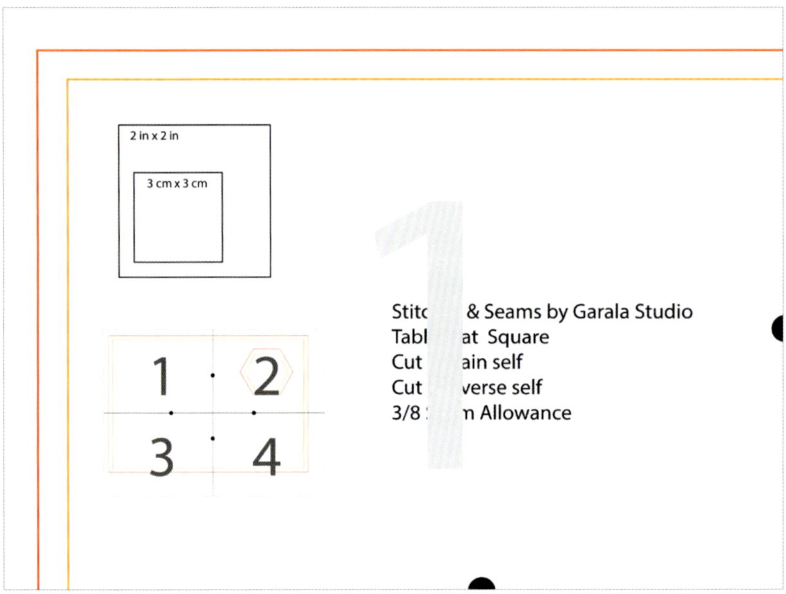

FIGURE 4.17C

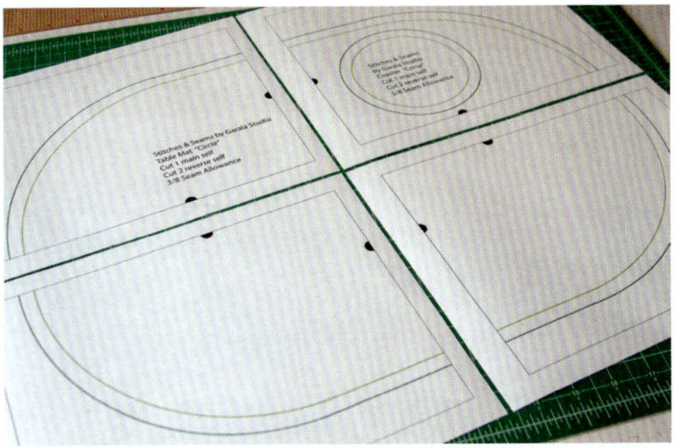

FIGURE 4.18A

FIGURE 4.18B

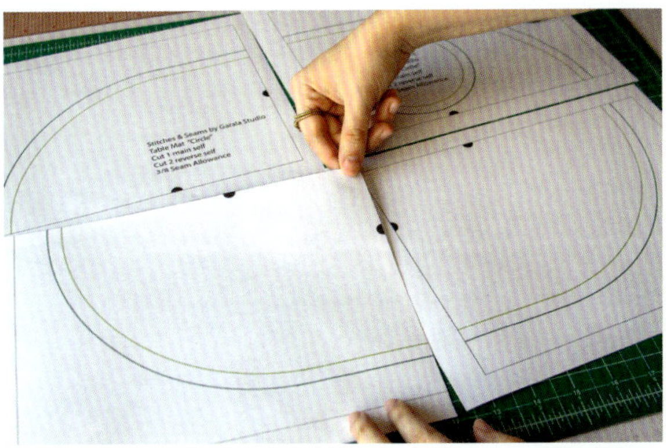

FIGURE 4.18C

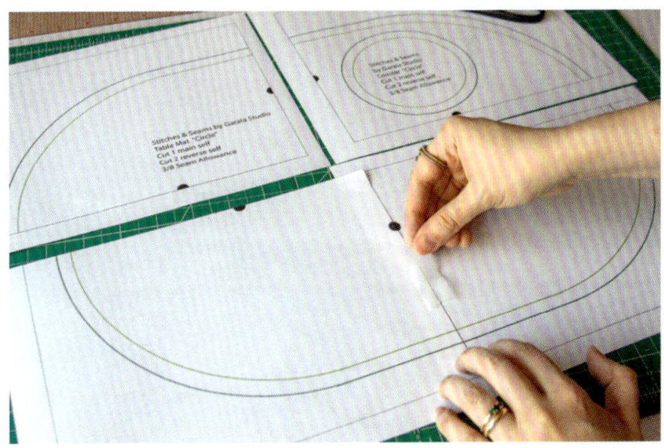

FIGURE 4.18D

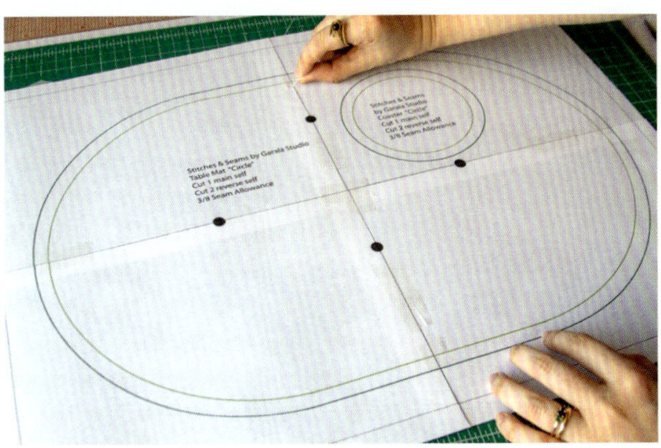

FIGURE 4.18E

Retracing

Step 1: Choose a lightweight and see-through paper. I suggest tissue paper but as long as you can see the pattern underneath it, you are good to go.

Step 2: Place your tracing paper on top of your pattern. You can follow the lines free-hand or with the aid of a ruler. If you need a larger paper to retrace a larger pattern, you can always add more with a bit of tape. (This is what I call little-cute-Frankenstein-patterns, and yes, we all do it at some point with the scraps from other patterns!)

Step 3: Add all the important info to your new, retraced piece (**FIGURE 4.19**).

Cutting Pattern Pieces onto Fabric

Step 1: Cut out all your paper pattern pieces. Pin them or secure them to the fabric with pattern weights (**FIGURE 4.20**).

Step 2: By either using fabric shears or a rotary cutter, cut the fabric as close to the edge of the pattern as you can.

Step 3: Mark all indicators such as notches, darts, etc. (**FIGURE 4.21**).

FIGURE 4.19

FIGURE 4.20

FIGURE 4.21

TIP If your fabric pieces are hanging together by a thread, do not pull your fabric away to rip the tiny threads. It is better to do another passing with your cutting tool. Otherwise you risk puckering your fabric.

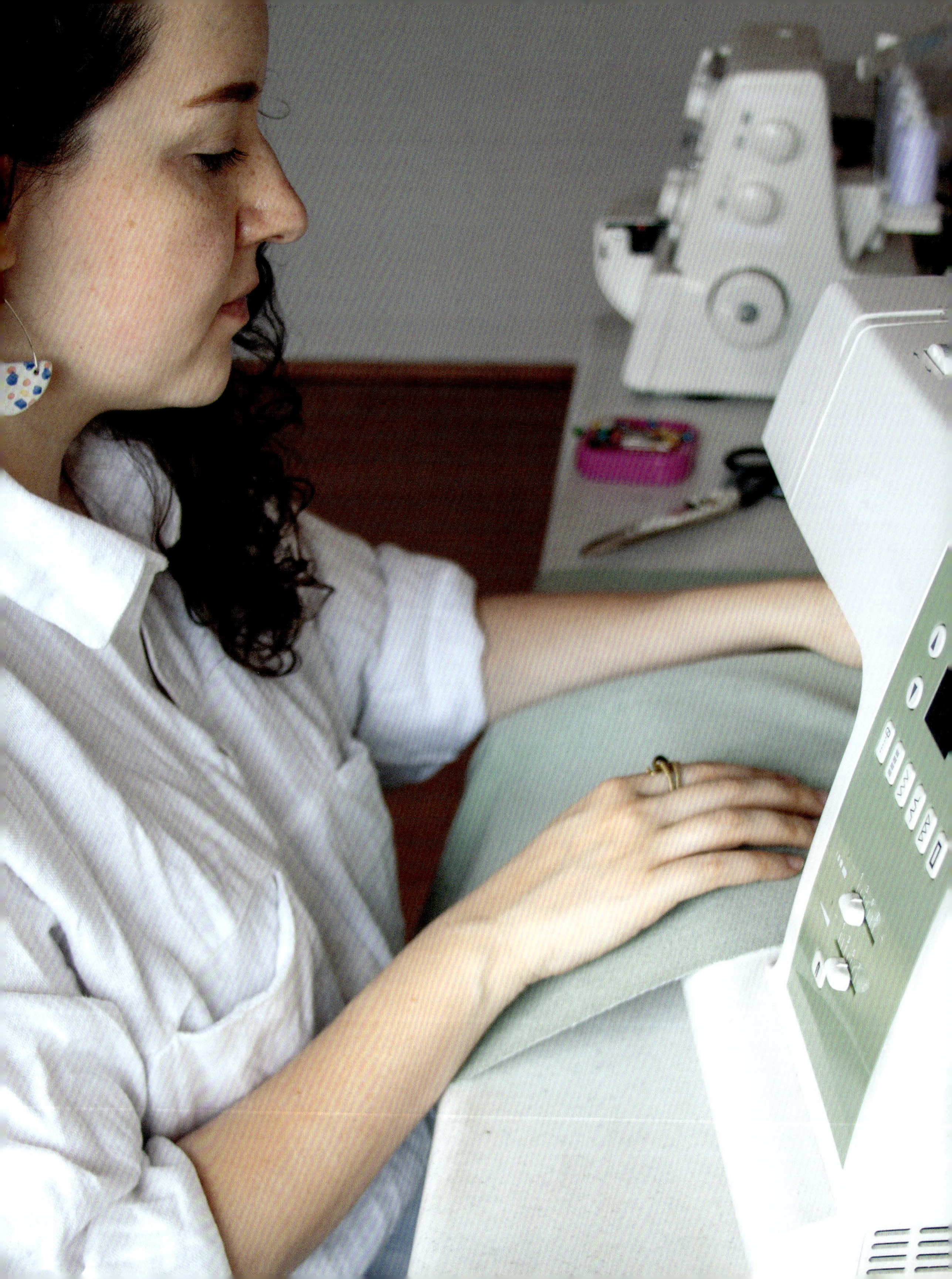

CHAPTER 5

Sewing Basics: Practice Makes Progress

LET'S GET SEWING

Alright, enough with the theory and on with the first practical sewing exercises.

FOR THE FOLLOWING SECTION YOU'LL NEED:

- Sewing machine
- Universal sewing needles (I recommend size 9/14)
- Six fabric squares measuring 8x8 inches (20x20 centimeters) (I suggest unbleached cotton muslin)
- Polyester thread, in a contrasting color to your chosen fabric
- Pencil
- Straight ruler
- Square ruler (optional)
- Fabric shears (pinking shears optional)

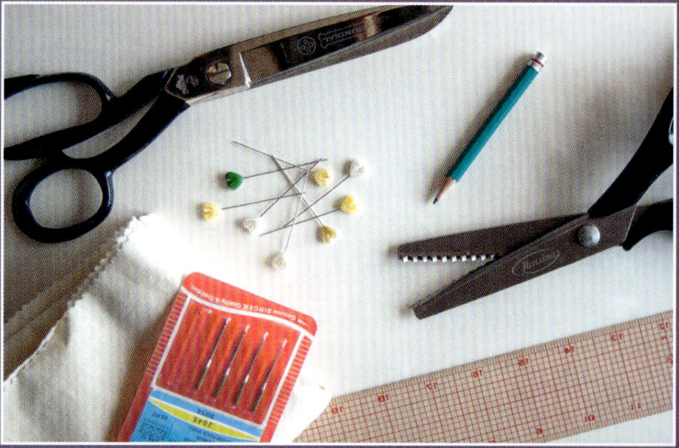

PREP WORK

1. Begin by creating your seven 8x8-inch squares (make sure they are perfectly straight). (Optionally, you can cut your squares using pinking shears.)
2. Switch on your sewing machine and set it to straight stitch. Make sure you've loaded your bobbin into the machine.
3. Read the entire instructions for each exercise before you sew. This way you'll get ready and plan accordingly how to act at the sewing machine.

MY SECRET SAUCE

To see this in action, visit the video gallery at rockynook.com/sewing_videos.

This is what I call the few steps I do right before starting to stitch my seams. These steps have long ensured I always make neat seams, and if you adopt them as part of your ritual, I am sure they will be magic for you, too.

1. At the machine, pull both threads from the needle plate (the spool and the bobbin) to the back and leave them long and hanging (**FIGURE 5.1**).

2. Place your fabric underneath the presser foot and put it down (**FIGURE 5.2**).

3. Using the manual wheel, do your first couple of stitches manually (**FIGURE 5.3**). (This secures the thread to the fabric, ensuring you'll start a correct row of stitches without jammed thread or knots).

4. Back tack (**FIGURE 5.4**). You can now start your seam properly. Gently press the foot controller to start stitching.

   The hanging threads at the back work magic when a bulky seam refuses to go through the feeding dogs. By gently pulling the threads (which are now tied to the fabric because of your first manual stitches), you help the fabric to slide backward without the fuss of directly pulling on it.

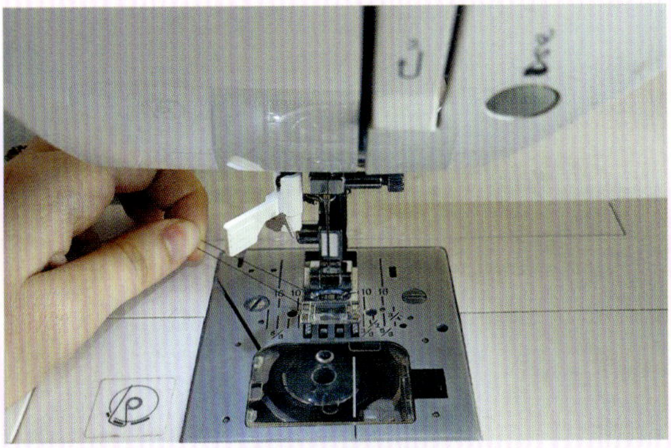

FIGURE 5.1

FIGURE 5.2

FIGURE 5.3

FIGURE 5.4

STRAIGHT LINES WITH A STRAIGHT STITCH

1. Pick one of the 8x8-inch fabric squares. Draw straight lines on it from edge to edge with pencil starting at ½ inch from the right edge of the square.
2. Draw more straight, parallel lines toward the opposite edge of the square, varying them in separation (**FIGURE 5.5**). This is the grid you'll follow.
3. Place the top edge of the first line you drew under the presser foot, leaving about ⅛ inch at the top (**FIGURE 5.6**). This is to ensure your first stitch catches the fabric. With practice you'll achieve starting at the very edge of the material.
4. Set the presser foot down.
5. Move the needle manually to confirm it hits the pencil line. Do the first couple of stitches manually with your hand wheel.
6. Gently step on your foot control to begin stitching.
7. Go slowly and guide your fabric with your hands gently. Remember, the feed dogs move the fabric backward, there is no need for you to pull or push. Simply focus on guiding.

TIP As you are stitching, try to keep the fabric edge following the seam allowance guideline on your machine instead of focusing on the needle through the drawn line. For me, following the needle leads to wobbly seams because I lose sight of the whole area; whereas, following seam allowance guidelines ensures I am keeping the required seam allowance throughout the entire seam. This is not to say that you'll never focus on the needle, you will for certain projects, but my advice is to start practicing by looking at the overall scene.

FIGURE 5.5

FIGURE 5.6

Do *gently guide.*

Don't *force the fabric to quickly change direction.*

8. Continue to the end of the drawn line at the lower edge of the square.
9. Lift the presser foot, pull your fabric out, and cut the threads (**FIGURE 5.7**).

Practice doing four or five lines this way. For the remaining lines, practice the back tack (the reverse stitch that secures the seam, detailed in the next exercise). Thus, you'll see the difference between a back tack seam and a regular seam in the same sample (**FIGURE 5.8**).

> **TIP** I like to cut the threads with my clippers instead of using the machine's thread cutter because the thread cutter is behind the machine, and I feel like there's more thread waste using it.

FIGURE 5.7

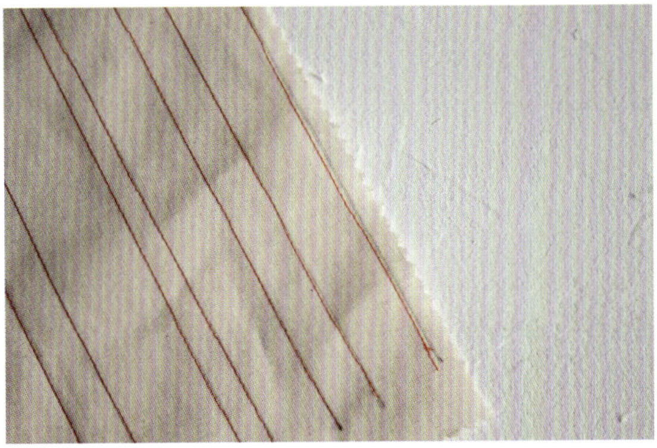

FIGURE 5.8

BACK TACK

1. Put the fabric in place under the presser foot.

2. Make just the first couple of stitches manually.

3. Do three more forward stitches (automatically with your foot controller). Now it's time to make the back tack. Some machines do this automatically with the touch of a button (**FIGURE 5.9**), and some machines require pushing the reverse stitch button in concert with the foot controller. Back tack until you reach the very first stitch at the top edge of the fabric.

TIP The regular motion of (forward) stitching pulls your fabric backward. A reverse stitch will bring the fabric toward you for as long as you press the reverse button.

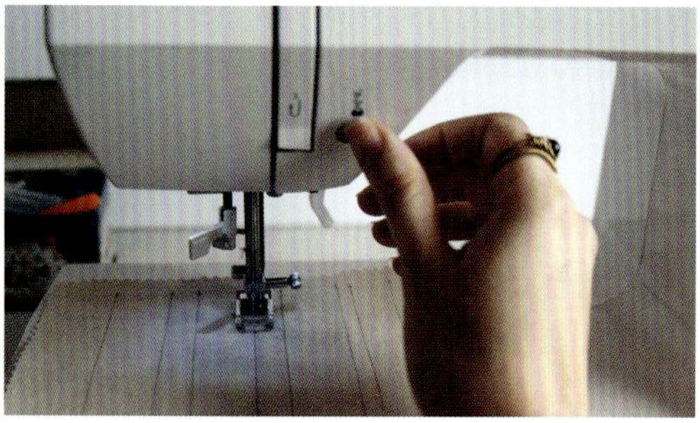

FIGURE 5.9

4. Release the reverse stitch button and continue pressing the foot controller. This will resume the regular motion of forward stitches, pulling the fabric backward again.

5. Complete the entire seam like before.

FIGURE 5.10 *The first line of stitches on the left has no back tack. The second and fourth lines have back tacking, but the threads were not pulled to the back before sewing, creating a knot. The third line has back tack and the threads were hanging to the back of the machine, so it has a clean first stitch.*

Optional: If your sewing machine has adjustable length and width for the stitches, practice doing more straight lines varying the length of your stitch. You can try a very long one (for a basting stitch, for instance) or a super short one.

STRAIGHT LINES WITH ZIGZAG STITCH

1. Repeat steps 1–4 from the straight stitch exercise.

2. Set your stitch to default zigzag without making any adjustments to width or length.

3. Do the first couple of stitches manually with your hand wheel. You'll see the straight line you drew ends up right in the middle of the zigzag.

4. Back tack.

5. Complete the entire seam.

6. Release your fabric. If your sewing machine has an adjustable zigzag stitch, it can vary immensely in both length and width.

Practice doing different adjustments for the remaining lines to complete the square sample. In case your machine has more than one zigzag stitch, like lightning stitch or 3-step zigzag stitch, try those as well (**FIGURE 5.11**).

> **TIP** Don't rush your machine. The zigzag stitch tends to be a bit slower. Honor the pace of the feeding dogs, they'll get you there.

FIGURE 5.11 *From left to right: 3-step zigzag stitch, a regular zigzag stitch with increased width and decreased length between stitches (notice the puckering inside the stitches; this is due to the tension of the upper thread being off), a narrow zigzag, the default zigzag stitch with back tack at the beginning, and a default zigzag stitch with no back tack.*

> **TIP** Some uses for the zigzag stitch are finishing raw edges of fabric, sewing stretch fabric and elastics, gathering, sewing bartacks (a heavier stitch used as reinforcement on certain areas of a garment, like in jean's pockets), and decoration.

STRAIGHT PIVOT

Pivoting is by far my favorite sewing technique. It's so simple, yet I feel like such a master whenever I do one that it is a must for me to show it. This skill is useful for uninterrupted seams in anything with a square angle, like shirt collars, pillowcases, or corner facings.

1. Draw a squared spiral onto your fabric. Keep at least a ½ inch between lines (**FIGURE 5.12**).

2. Set your machine to straight stitch.

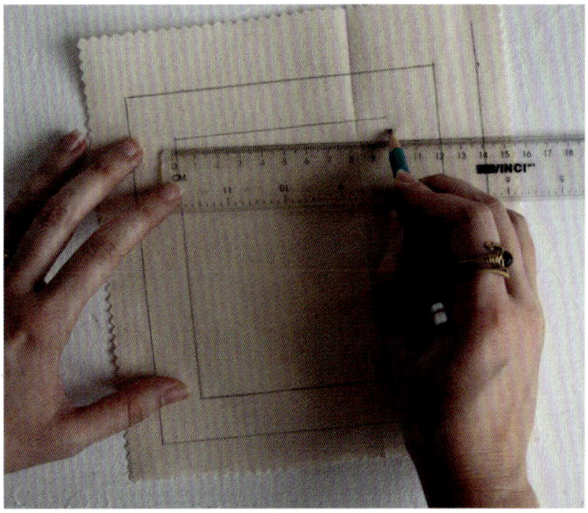

FIGURE 5.12

FIGURE 5.13

FIGURE 5.14

3. Place the start of your spiral under the presser foot, confirm the needle hits the drawn line, do the first couple of stitches manually, and back tack.

4. Sew by pressing the foot controller and follow the line (**FIGURE 5.13**).

5. About ¼ inch before reaching the first right angle, stop pressing the foot controller, switch to the hand wheel, and manually stitch your way toward the corner.

> **TIP** With practice you'll be able to reach the right angle with the automatic stitch with the foot controller, but for now do it manually so you see where the needle is going to hit.

6. Make sure the needle lands precisely on the 90° angle (**FIGURE 5.14**).

> **TIP** If you are not quite hitting the mark, lift the presser foot and adjust the fabric, whether you need it a bit back or forth. Since it'll be an adjustment of less than ⅛ inch, it won't be detrimental to your seam. The main thing here is to get crisp corners.

7. With the needle down securing the fabric at the right angle, lift your presser foot and pivot the fabric so you can keep on sewing a continuous seam on the next straight line (**FIGURE 5.15A–D**).

8. Repeat each time you reach the next squared angle to complete the spiral (**FIGURE 5.16A–B**).

9. Upon reaching the center, lift the presser foot and release the fabric.

FIGURE 5.15A

FIGURE 5.15B

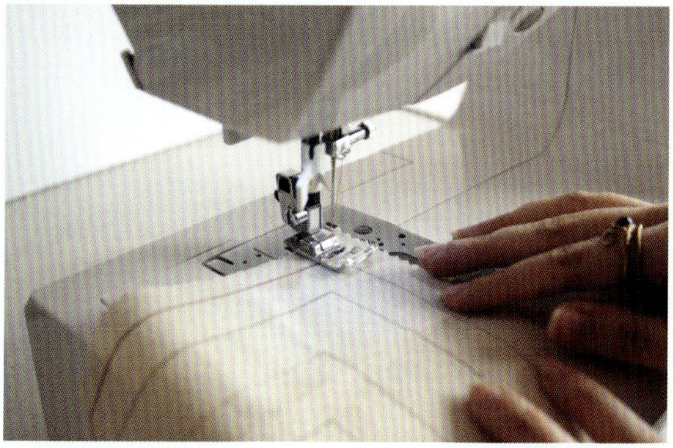
FIGURE 5.15C

FIGURE 5.15D

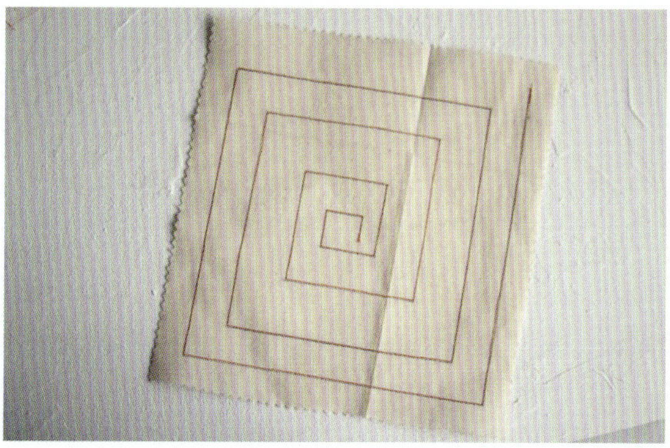
FIGURE 5.16A

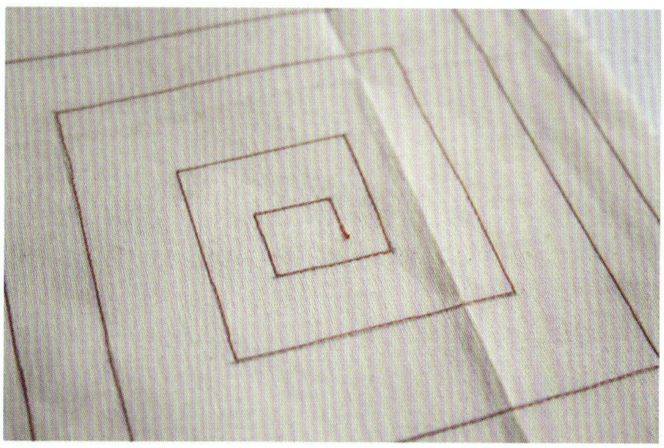
FIGURE 5.16B

WAVY LINES WITH A STRAIGHT STITCH

1. Draw wavy lines with your pencil starting ½ inch from the left edge of the square. Try not to make the waves too steep!
2. Trace more wavy lines toward the right edge, 1 inch from each other. This is the grid you'll follow.
3. Place the top edge of the first line you drew under the presser foot.
4. Set the presser foot down.
5. Move the needle manually to confirm it hits the pencil line.
6. Do the first couple of stitches manually with your hand wheel.
7. Gently step onto your foot control.
8. Go slowly! Guide your fabric with relaxed hands so the needle follows the curves.

> **TIP** Stop and readjust when needed. Remember to put your needle down to secure the fabric and lift the presser foot to shift the fabric—this way, even after readjusting the fabric, the next stitch will still be aligned with the previous one, creating a seamless look while still enabling you to follow the curved line.

9. Continue to the end of the drawn line at the lower edge.
10. Lift the presser foot, remove your fabric and cut the threads (**FIGURE 5.17**).

FIGURE 5.17 *From left to right: A wavy line where I didn't pivot enough (notice the sudden change in direction, creating pointy angles); the middle line most resembles a wavy line in a garment: flowy and gentle with no sudden changes; a wavy line with lots of pivots that looks almost seamless, but it's too steep for a regular garment.*

MATCHING TWO SIDES TOGETHER

When sewing clothing, this is the type of seam you'll do the most. Following the instructions for each project, you'll see how to join the fabric pieces together. In this case, we are matching fabric pieces with the right sides together. That means that the sides of the fabric you want to show on the outside of the garment are touching (this leads to the raw edge and seam allowance being concealed on the inside of the garment).

1. Put your two pieces of fabric right sides together, perfectly matching the edges (**FIGURE 5.18**).
2. Place both layers under the presser foot as you've done for the previous exercises.
3. Set the fabric to line up with a ⅝-inch seam allowance. Back tack at the very beginning. Then sew forward with a straight stitch (**FIGURE 5.19**).
4. Go slowly to really get familiar with how the two pieces pass through the machine together.
5. Make sure both layers are stable and stitched at the required seam allowance.
6. Back tack once you reach the other end of the seam.
7. Release your fabric and see how straight your seam is, as well as how it looks from the right side (**FIGURE 5.20A**) and the wrong side (**FIGURE 5.20B**).

FIGURE 5.18

FIGURE 5.19

FIGURE 5.20A

FIGURE 5.20B

SINGER

CHAPTER 6

Sewing Projects

LET'S GET CREATIVE!

The following supplies and instructions are your base for the next exercises. The additional materials and steps will be listed for each particular project.

SUPPLIES

- Sewing machine
- Universal sewing needles (I recommend size 9/14)
- Tape measure
- Iron press
- Sewing pins
- Tailor's chalk (or anything washable to make markings)
- Fabric shears
- Paper scissors
- Pencil
- Straight ruler
- Tape
- Optional: Rotary cutter, pattern weights, cutting mat

BASE INSTRUCTIONS

1. Print and assemble your sewing pattern (see page 77).
2. Retrace your pattern if needed.
3. Prewash and dry your fabric. (If any shrinkage should occur in the fabric, it is better to have it happen in this step rather than later on once the garment is fully sewn.)
4. Cut all your pattern pieces out of your fabric (see page 80).

IMPORTANT INFO Each of these PDF Sewing patterns comes in color because I wanted to showcase the seam allowances in case you want to make any adjustments. You'll see the inner shapes are the final size of the object, and the outer line is where you'll cut the piece onto fabric. The space between them is ⅜ inch.

PROJECT 1 PLACEMAT AND COASTER SET

For your first usable sewing project we will create a set of two-sided placemats and coasters. I created two options, the first and easiest is the rectangular set, and if you feel confident enough to turn it up a notch, I also created the circular version. The only difference is that with the first option, you'll only practice straight lines—with the latter option, you get to practice sewing soft curves.

For this exercise I will be sewing the entire circular set. The steps are the same for all pieces of the set, whether you are doing the circular or the rectangular.

WHAT YOU'LL NEED

- Base supplies
- PDF sewing pattern (Download at rockynook.com/sewing_patterns)
- Fabric A (I suggest a print): 1 yd, 59 in (150 cm) wide
- Fabric B (I suggest a solid for contrast): 1 yd, 59 in (150 cm) wide
- Matching polyester thread (I will sew with a contrasting thread so it is more visible for you, but this also brings a nice topstitch quality to the finished piece if you wish to try it.)

This material list will yield six sets.

FABRIC SUGGESTIONS

Choose a lightweight woven fabric that presses well like cotton lawn, poplin, or chambray. It's better in this situation to refrain from using stretchy materials.

FOR ALL SEAMS Seam allowance is ⅜ inch. Back tack at the beginning and end of each seam and cut all loose threads (unless a certain step says otherwise).

CUTTING LIST

For this project you need to have, for each set:

- Placemat (piece 1)—cut 1 from main fabric (A)
- Placemat (piece 1)—cut 1 from contrast/reverse fabric (B)
- Coaster (piece 2)—cut 1 from main fabric (A)
- Coaster (piece 2)—cut 1 from contrast/reverse fabric (B)

SKILL SET

This project will help you practice:

- Straight seams with straight stitch
- Topstitch (very common in garment construction)
- Sewing soft curves (in the case of circular placemat)
- Angular pivots (in the case of the rectangular placemat) useful for collars, corners, and cushions

FIGURE 6.1.1 *All four pieces of fabric*

FIGURE 6.1.2 *Match the two sets of pieces together, right sides together.*

Step 1: Assembling the Placemat

Once you have the fabric pieces cut, grab all the pieces needed for one set (four pieces: a front and back placemat and a front and back coaster) (**FIGURE 6.1.1**). Make sure you clipped the notches on the placemat.

Starting with the placemat, set the two pieces of fabric right sides together on top of each other matching their shapes (**FIGURE 6.1.2**). Secure with sewing pins, leaving an opening between the notches (this won't be sewn) (**FIGURE 6.1.3**). I like to signal mine with a different color of sewing pin (**FIGURE 6.1.4**).

FIGURE 6.1.3 *Secure with pins*

FIGURE 6.1.4 *Mark your notches!*

FIGURE 6.1.6 *Leave a gap to turn the placemat inside out.*

Step 2: Joining the Pieces Together

At the machine, practice my secret sauce: secure your fabric in place with the presser foot, pull threads to the back, do your first couple of stitches manually, back tack, and you are ready to go.

Sew the two layers together at a 3/8-inch seam allowance starting at the first sewing pin signaling the opening at the notch (**FIGURE 6.1.5**). You will leave an unstitched gap between the notches so you are able to turn the placemat right sides out later on (**FIGURE 6.1.6**). It is very important to back tack at the beginning and end of the seam to secure the gap from ripping open (**FIGURE 6.1.7**).

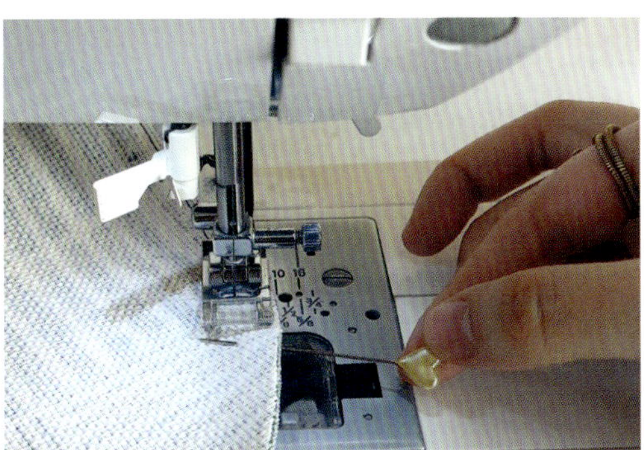

FIGURE 6.1.5 *Set at a 3/8 inch seam allowance*

FIGURE 6.1.7 *The finished seam*

Remove sewing pins before they pass under the presser foot and needle.

> **TIP** If you need to readjust the fabric at the curve, put your needle down to secure the continuity of the stitch, release your presser foot, and pivot the fabric.
>
> *To see this in action, visit the video gallery at rockynook.com/sewing_videos.*

Step 3: Right Sides Out

Clip the curved seam allowances (**FIGURE 6.1.8**). Turn the placemat inside out through the gap (**FIGURE 6.1.9**).

FIGURE 6.1.8 *Clip the curves.*

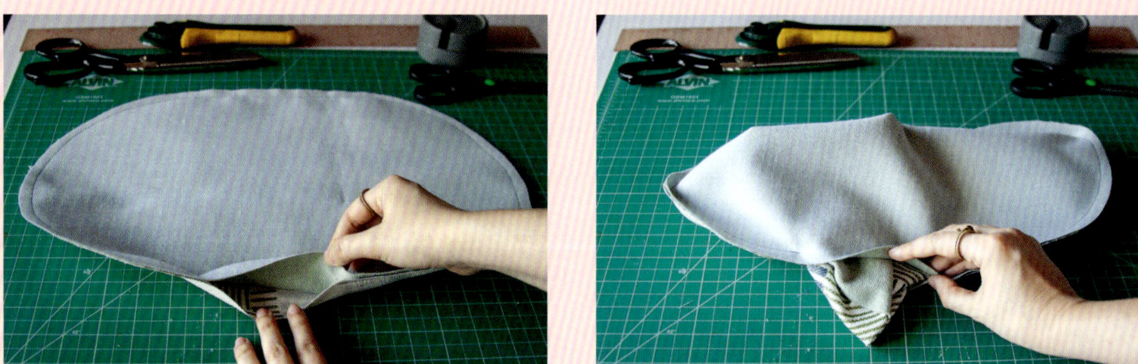

FIGURE 6.1.9 *Turn it inside out at the gap.*

Step 4: Pressing the Seams

With a pointy tool (I chose a pencil) (**FIGURE 6.1.10**), poke the seam allowances toward the edge from the inside to really get a crisp shape. I even roll the fabric away from the seam (**FIGURE 6.1.11**). Then iron press to keep it flat and neat (**FIGURE 6.1.12**). By pressing, the unstitched gap will naturally fold the raw edges of the seam allowance inside.

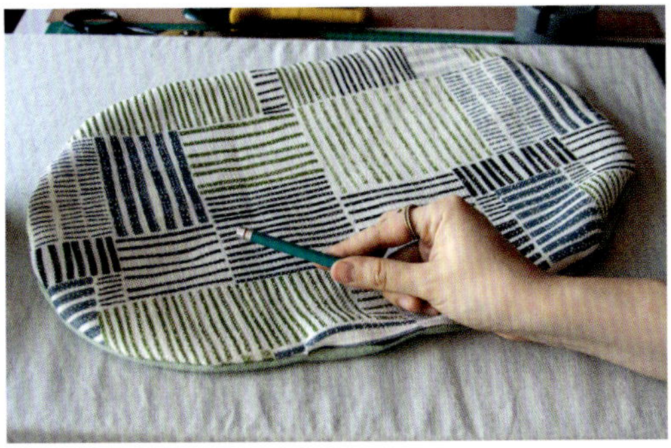

FIGURE 6.1.10 *Use a pencil to push the mat into shape.*

FIGURE 6.1.11 *Roll the fabric away from the seam.*

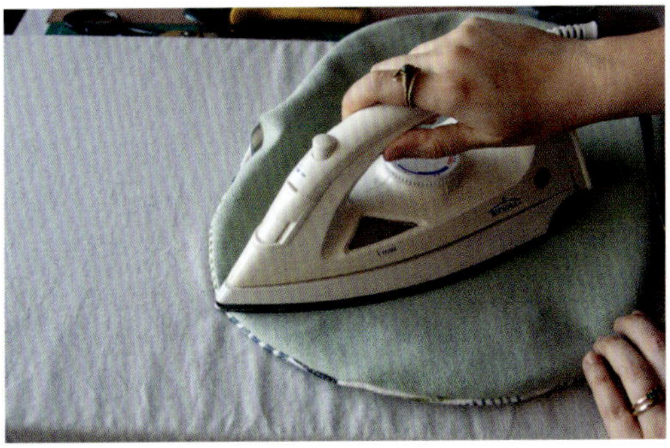

FIGURE 6.1.12 *Press.*

FIGURE 6.1.13 *The difference between a pressed seam and an unpressed (and unimpressed!) seam*

Step 5: Final Seams

Topstitch around the entire placemat to close the open gap and to secure that each side stays flat and won't peek onto the other (**FIGURE 6.1.14**). Topstitching is doing an additional and visible passing of stitches to secure or reinforce an already existing seam. Usually this is sewn closer to the edge (at about ⅛ inch or ¼ inch from the edge) (**FIGURE 6.1.15**). You can choose a contrasting thread to add detail (like in denim jeans) or matching thread for a seamless look (**FIGURE 6.1.16**).

Remember to back tack at the beginning and end to secure the seam (**FIGURE 6.1.17**). I suggest you start your seam by the closed edges, rather than start at the opening.

TIP It can be a good idea to paste a little tape as a guide onto your sewing machine to keep the visible topstitch extra straight.

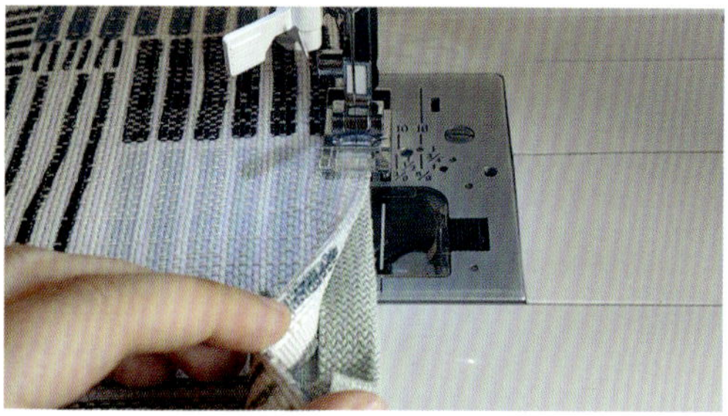

FIGURE 6.1.14 *Topstitch to close the gap.*

FIGURE 6.1.15 *Sew at ⅛ or ¼ inch.*

FIGURE 6.1.16 *Black thread is visible, but matches the fabric.*

FIGURE 6.1.17 *Back tack on either side of the seam.*

Step 6: Assembling the Coasters

Repeat the steps to sew the coaster. Since this is a smaller shape, you'll need to pivot frequently to meet the curve; just remember to put your needle down before you lift the presser foot. Likewise, I like to secure the open gap with sewing pins when pressing and sewing these smaller coasters (**FIGURES 6.1.18A–D**).

To see this in action, visit the video gallery at rockynook.com/sewing_videos.

FIGURE 6.1.18A

FIGURE 6.1.18B

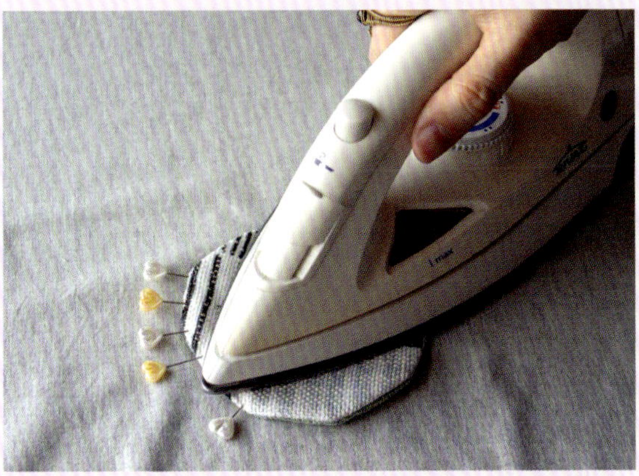

FIGURE 6.1.18C

FIGURE 6.1.18D

The steps for the angular placemat and coaster are the same, the only difference being the angular pivot at each corner (**FIGURE 6.1.19**). To get those corners super pointy, trim the excess seam allowance at each angle (be careful not to snip any stitches!) (**FIGURE 6.1.20**) and poke the seams out from the inside just like with the circle.

FIGURE 6.1.19 *Angular pivots*

FIGURE 6.1.20 *Trim seam allowances*

FIGURE 6.1.21 *The final product!*

PROJECT 2 TOTE BAG

This tote bag is an everyday bag with multiple pockets that will help us practice garment construction. Unlike a flat item (like the placemat set), this tote bag will expand your understanding of how two-dimensional pattern pieces transform into a three-dimensional wearable piece. The multiple pieces of this tote bag open the possibilities for different fabric combos, topstitching, or visual effects from the different colors. Feel free to experiment!

WHAT YOU'LL NEED

- Base supplies (see page 96)
- PDF sewing pattern (Download at rockynook.com/sewing_patterns)
- Main fabric A (I am using pink): 1 yd, 59 inch (150 cm) wide
- Contrast fabric B (I am using brown): ½ yd, 59 inch (150 cm) wide
- Matching polyester thread (I will sew with a contrasting thread so it is more visible for you, but this also brings a nice topstitch quality to the finished piece if you wish to try it.)

FABRIC SUGGESTIONS

Choose a medium-weight woven fabric that presses well, like canvas, lightweight denim, lawn, twill, or gabardine. It's better in this situation to refrain from stretchy materials.

CUTTING LIST

For this project you need to have:

- Main canvas (piece 1)—cut 2 from main fabric (A)
- Bottom (piece 2)—cut 1 from main fabric (A)
- Full pocket (piece 3)—cut 1 from main fabric (A)
- Front mini pocket (piece 4)—cut 1 from contrasting fabric (B)
- Facing (piece 5)—cut 2 from main fabric (A)
- Straps (piece 6)—cut 4 from contrasting fabric ON FOLD (B)
- Inside mini pocket, full (piece 7)—cut 1 from main fabric (A)
- Inside mini pocket, lower flap (piece 8)—cut 1 from main fabric (A)
- Inside mini pocket, upper flap (piece 9)—cut 1 from main fabric (A)
- A fabric strip cut on the bias measuring 15x1 in (40x2.5 cm)

You can also choose to cut the pieces on different fabric depending on the color combo you wish to have.

FOR ALL SEAMS The seam allowance is ⅜ inch. Back tack at the beginning and end of each seam and cut all loose threads (unless a certain step says otherwise).

SKILL SET

This project will help you practice:

- Hong Kong seams
- French seams
- Iron press
- Varying seam allowances
- Facings
- Stitch in the ditch

Step 1: Cut Your Pattern Pieces

Start with cutting your fabric according to the paper patterns (**FIGURE 6.2.1**).

For the main basket canvas (piece 1) which requires two identical pieces of fabric, I cut it with the fabric folded even if I don't need it "on the fold" (this yields two symmetrical, mirrored pieces with one cut) (**FIGURE 6.2.2**). With time you'll see that usually you need two of most pieces because garments commonly need two sleeves, two legs, two pockets, two sides, and so on.

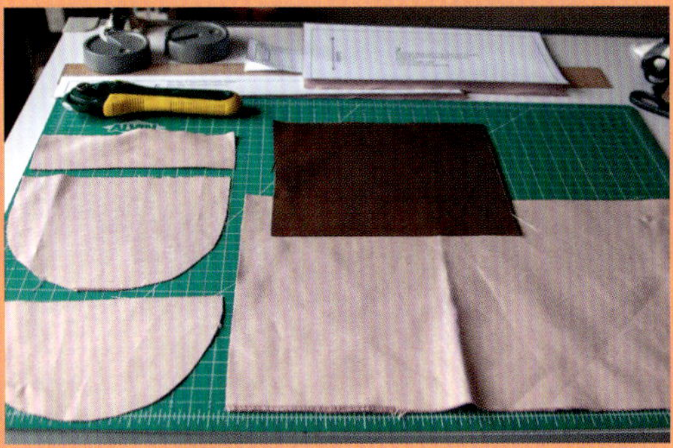

FIGURE 6.2.1

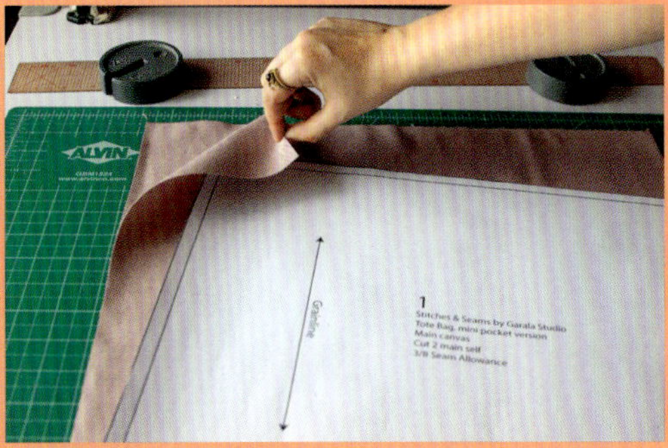

FIGURE 6.2.2

Step 2: Assembling the Inside Mini Pocket

To preserve the integrity of the pocket, we'll create a Hong Kong seam (similar to bias tape, but fancier!). A Hong Kong seam is a type of finishing where an additional strip of fabric is wrapped around a raw edge, usually in a contrasting fabric to the main material. It is cut on the bias for added give and stretch. In this case, the additional strip of fabric will wrap around the edges of pieces 8 and 9 (inside mini pocket flaps) to preserve the raw edge from unraveling (**FIGURE 6.2.3**).

Right sides together, stitch the strip to the flat straight edge of pieces 8 and 9 with a ¼-in seam allowance (**FIGURE 6.2.4**). Iron press the fabric strip away from the main pocket (**FIGURE 6.2.5**) and then toward the wrong side of the pocket, wrapping the raw edge of the main fabric (**FIGURES 6.2.6A–C**).

FIGURE 6.2.3

FIGURE 6.2.4

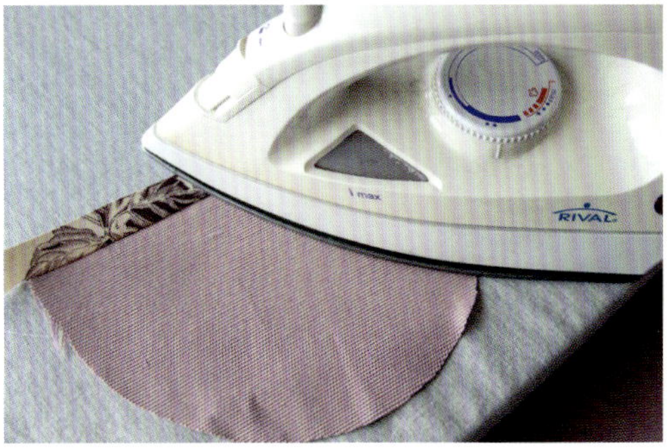

FIGURE 6.2.5

FIGURE 6.2.6A

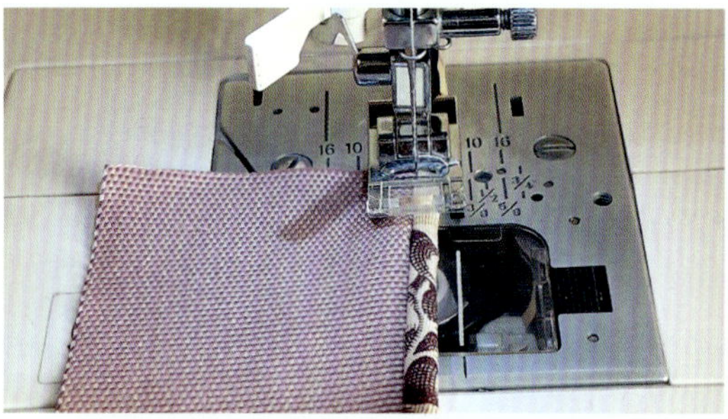

FIGURE 6.2.6B

FIGURE 6.2.6C

Place it under the presser foot with the right side facing up. Aim to stitch right where both fabrics meet on the existing seam—this is called a stitch in the ditch (**FIGURE 6.2.7**). The seam will be visible from the wrong side, but disappears from the right side.

To see this in action, visit the video gallery at rockynook.com/sewing_videos.

FIGURE 6.2.7

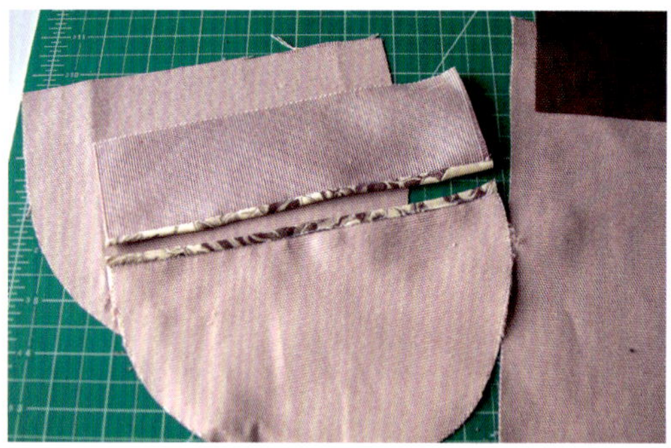

FIGURE 6.2.8

Overlap piece 9 on top of piece 8, right sides facing up, and then cover them both with piece 7, right sides together, making sure all edges match exactly (**FIGURE 6.2.9**). Pin in place and sew the curved edge with a straight stitch at ⅜ in, leaving the top straight edge open (**FIGURE 6.2.10**).

FIGURE 6.2.9

FIGURE 6.2.10

Step 3: Assembling the Remaining Pockets (Pieces 3 and 4)

Fold the top edge (one of the wider sides) of each piece to the wrong side ¼ inch (**FIGURE 6.2.11**), iron press, and stitch as close to the edge as you can—then, fold under, press, and stitch again close to the edge (**FIGURE 6.2.12**). This will result in one seam from the right side and two parallel seams from the wrong side (**FIGURE 6.2.13**). The sides and bottom will remain with raw unfinished edges. This is a very simple finish to prevent raw edges from fraying. Now, all pockets are ready (**FIGURE 6.2.14**).

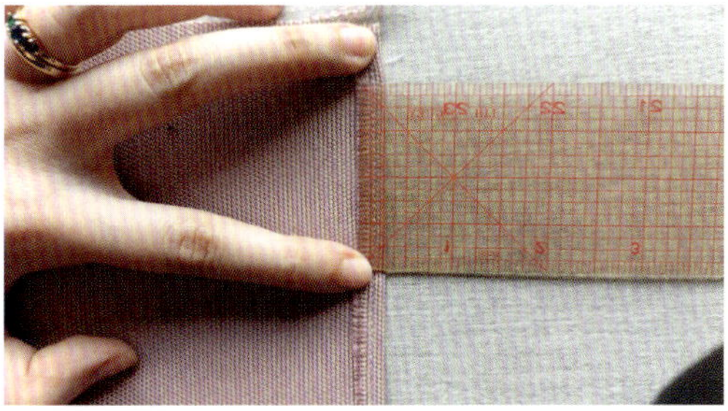

FIGURE 6.2.11

FIGURE 6.2.12

FIGURE 6.2.13

FIGURE 6.2.14

Step 4: Assembling the Straps

Each strap (piece 6) consists of two pieces of fabric sewn together to keep raw edges hidden inside. Fold and press just one lengthwise edge towards the wrong side of your fabric at ¼ inch. Do this to all four fabric strips (**FIGURE 6.2.15**).

TIP To ensure even, lengthwise folds: Double the amount you need to fold, and trace it to the wrong side of the fabric with a ruler. Then make the raw edge and the traced line match, pin in place, and fold. Example: If you need a ¼-inch fold, trace the line at ½ inch from the raw edge of the fabric.

Join a pair of straps right sides together and sew (at the unfolded edge) with straight stitch at ⅜ inch. Repeat with the remaining pair of straps (**FIGURE 6.2.16**).

Turn the straps inside out and press the seam to keep it right on the edge, (poke with a pointy tool if necessary). When pressing, be careful not to flatten the previously folded edges, which are now toward the wrong side/inside (**FIGURE 6.2.17**).

FIGURE 6.2.15

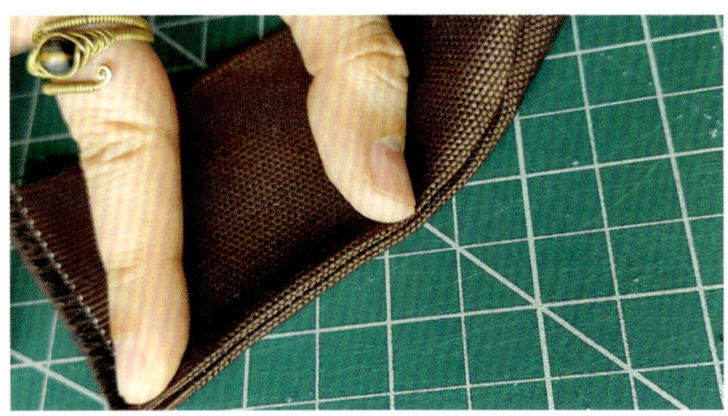

FIGURE 6.2.16

FIGURE 6.2.17

FIGURE 6.2.18

FIGURE 6.2.19

Topstitch to close the opening, stitching as close as you can to the edge (**FIGURE 2.6.18**). You can choose a contrasting thread to give it a more utilitarian feel, or sew with a matching thread to create a seamless strap (**FIGURE 2.6.19**). Leave the ends raw, they will be sewn inside the tote bag so no fraying will occur.

Step 5: Joining the Straps to the Bag

Find the center front of pieces 1, 3, and 4. Pin to mark. Match and overlap the centers of all three pieces, and pin in place (**FIGURE 2.6.20A–B**).

Put one strap on top, aligning the bottom raw edges and ensuring the raw side of the pocket matches with the center of the strap. Repeat with the other side and back side (that has no pockets). Pin in place and sew with a straight stitch as close to the edge as you can to secure all lengthwise sides of the straps to the bag and pockets (dotted yellow line) (**FIGURE 6.2.21A–B**). Stop and back tack 2 in (5 cm) (blue line) before the top edge of the main pocket (piece 3).

FIGURE 6.2.20A

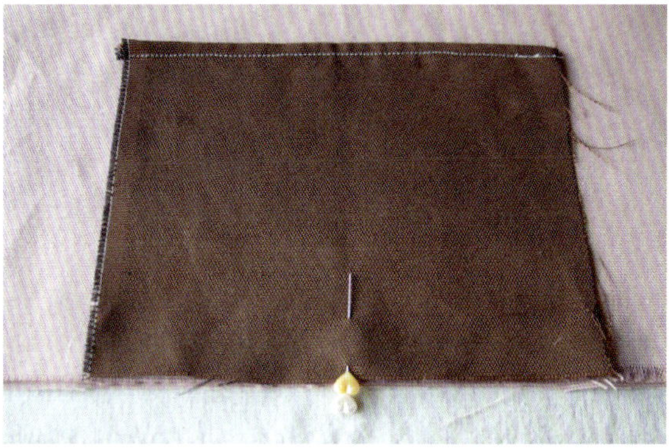

FIGURE 6.2.20B

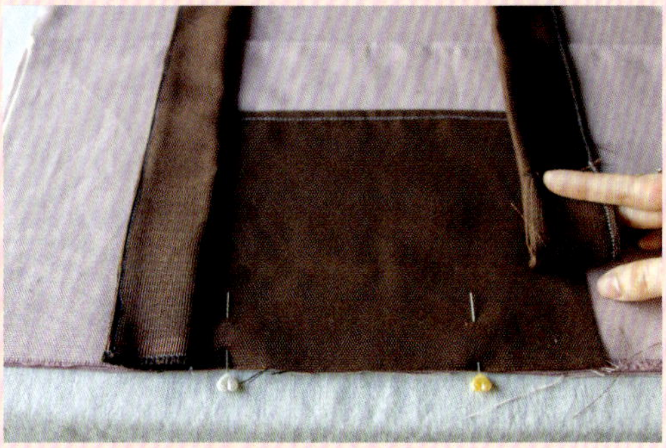

FIGURE 6.2.21A

FIGURE 6.2.21B

Step 6: Sewing the Base with French Seams

Place the back (piece 1—it has no pockets) with the wrong side facing up. Find its center back and mark it with a pin at the bottom. Find the center of the bottom piece (piece 2) and mark it with a pin (**FIGURE 6.2.22**).

Overlap the pins to match both centers and add more pins to secure both layers together. Add the inside mini pocket on the top edge of piece 1 between the straps. Pin everything in place and stitch together at ¼ in with a straight stitch. This is the first passing of two, to complete the French seam.

FIGURE 6.2.22

Repeat with the front (piece 1), sewing it to the bottom piece (**FIGURE 6.2.23**). Trim the seam allowances down to ⅛ in (**FIGURE 6.2.24**).

FIGURE 6.2.23

FIGURE 6.2.24

Step 7: Closing Side Seams with French Seams

Fold the bag so the raw seam allowances rest on the inside, and iron press so the seams rest right on the edge (**FIGURE 6.2.25**). With this "folded seam" facing outside, sew the second and final passing of the French seam at ⅜ in from the folded edge (**FIGURE 6.2.26A**). Make sure no loose threads are hanging from either side (**FIGURE 6.2.26B**).

FIGURE 6.2.25

FIGURE 6.2.26A

FIGURE 6.2.26B

Step 8: Closing the Bottom

Two small openings remain at both sides (**FIGURE 6.2.27**). These will be closed with a French seam, too. Match wrong sides together, aligning the raw edges, and stitch (with the right side of the bag on the outside) (**FIGURE 6.2.28**).

Sew again from the wrong side to conceal the raw edge. This bottom seam is what takes the two-dimensional pieces into a three-dimensional tote bag (**FIGURE 6.2.29A–E**).

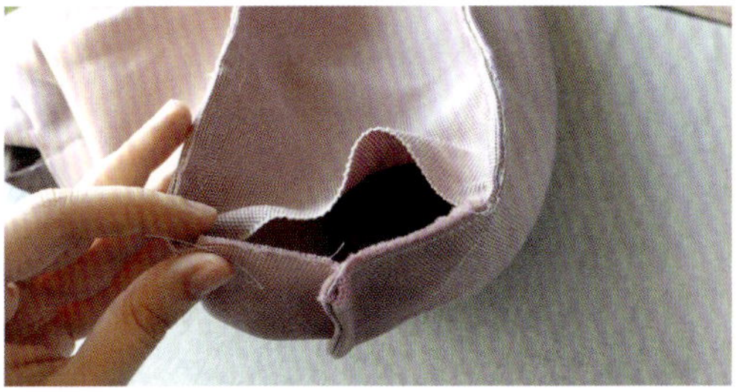

FIGURE 6.2.27

FIGURE 6.2.28

FIGURE 6.2.29A

FIGURE 6.2.29B

FIGURE 6.2.29C

FIGURE 6.2.29D *The bottom of the bag*

FIGURE 6.2.29E *The bottom of the bag, from the inside*

Step 9: Facings

Lastly, sew the remaining two pieces, the facings (piece 5). Right sides together, use a straight stitch at ⅜ in along the shorter raw edges, creating a loop (**FIGURE 6.2.30**).

FIGURE 6.2.30

Place the loop around the bag on the outside, right sides together, matching side seams and top raw edges (**FIGURE 6.2.31**). Pin in place. Stitch along that top raw edge with a straight stitch at ⅜ in.

Press toward the wrong side, making sure the seam rests right at the edge and press with a hot iron to keep in place (**FIGURE 6.2.32**). Fold under the remaining raw edge and topstitch to secure its position.

Optional: I like to also topstitch the upper edge to ensure there's no peeking over.

FIGURE 6.2.31

FIGURE 6.2.32

FIGURE 6.2.33
The final product!

PROJECT 3 ZIPPER POUCH

Take your sewing to the next level by learning how to add a zipper. This is a fundamental skill to construct a lot of garments so it will prove to be useful once you start sewing your own clothes. To practice this, we are creating a zipper pouch with a quilted base and a matching lining to enclose the raw edges of each pattern piece. Again, a three-dimensional piece will result from perfectly flat patterns.

WHAT YOU'LL NEED

- Base supplies (see page 96)
- PDF sewing pattern (Download at rockynook.com/sewing_patterns)
- Main fabric A (I am using a geometric print fabric): ½ yd, 59 in (150 cm) wide
- Contrast fabric B (I am using a solid green): ½ yd, 59 in (150 cm) wide
- Lining fabric C (I am using a beige linen): ½ yd, 59 in (150 cm) wide
- Filling/batting (optional) for a quilting look: ½ yd, 59 in (150 cm) wide
- 15-in (38-cm) zipper (In case you can't find this length, I'll show you how to adjust the pattern.)
- Zipper presser foot
- Matching polyester thread (I will sew with a contrasting thread so it is more visible for you, but this also brings a nice topstitch quality to the finished piece if you wish to try it).

FABRIC SUGGESTIONS

Outer Fabric: Choose a medium-weight woven fabric like canvas, lawn, twill, gabardine, poplin, or linen, or even experiment with lightweight pleather, mikado, or brocade. It's better in this situation to refrain from stretchy materials.

Inner Filling: Quilt batting, nylon foam, cut and sew foam, wad, or pellon

CUTTING LIST

For this project you need to have:

- Lower base piece (piece 1)—cut 1 from main fabric (A)
- Upper piece (piece 2)—cut 2 from contrasting fabric (B)
- Uni piece for lining (piece 3)—cut 1 ON FOLD from fabric (C)
- Inner filling (piece 4)—cut 1 from batting (D)

You can choose to cut the pieces on different fabrics depending on the color combo you wish to have.

FOR ALL SEAMS Seam allowance is ⅜ in. Back tack at the beginning and end of each seam and cut all loose threads (unless a certain step says otherwise).

SKILL SET

This project will help you practice:

- Zipper application
- Enclosed lining
- Quilting
- Straight stitch
- The use of right and wrong side of the fabric

Step 1: Adjusting the Length to Fit the Zipper

Oftentimes I don't find the exact zipper length or color or type to fit my project. Sometimes this means compromising to what's available—in this case, by adjusting the pattern to fit a larger zipper (**FIGURE 6.3.1**).

FIGURE 6.3.1

FIGURE 6.3.2

FIGURE 6.3.3

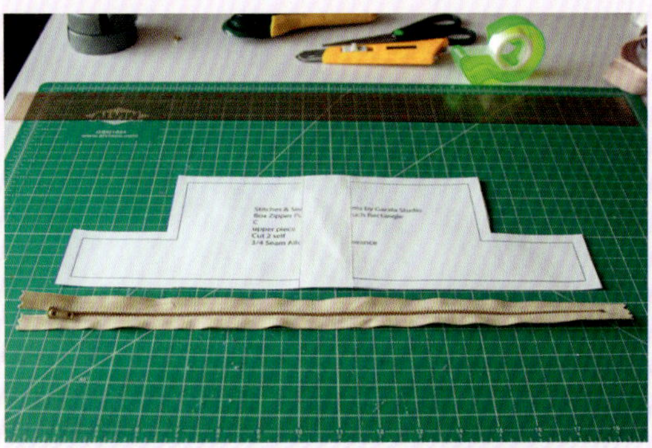

FIGURE 6.3.4

Start by tracing a straight line with a pencil perpendicular to the base line of the pattern (**FIGURE 6.3.2**). (For this exercise we are tracing it ourselves. This line is the self-made version of the "shorten or lengthen here" line most patterns include. In case they aren't included, this is how you can draft them yourself.) Cut along the line with your paper scissors (**FIGURE 6.3.3**). Later, you will paste an additional piece of paper to join both sides of the pattern and create a wider piece (**FIGURE 6.3.4**). The additional paper piece can be as wide as needed depending on how much larger the zipper is compared to the pattern piece.

The same can be done to subtract from the pattern, by cutting and overlapping the pieces to your desired size.

TIP Remember all pattern pieces need to be adjusted to match, so if you added 3 inches to piece 1 for instance, the rest of the pieces need to have the same adjustment (FIGURE 6.3.5).

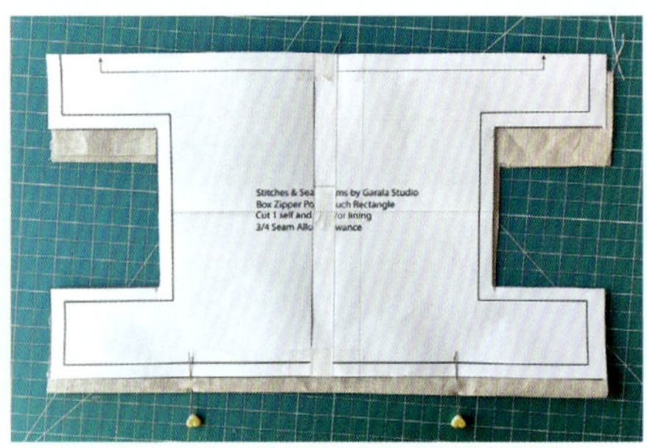

FIGURE 6.3.5

Step 2: Cutting the Fabric

Cut all your pattern pieces out of fabric. Pay close attention to the lining piece (piece 3). Transfer the notches from paper to fabric with the help of pins and cut an opening from notch to notch (**FIGURE 6.3.6A–C**). This opening will enable you to turn the final piece inside out. This opening is cut in the folded side.

FIGURE 6.3.6A

FIGURE 6.3.6B

FIGURE 6.3.6C

Step 3: Assembling the Outer Layer

With all fabric pieces cut (**FIGURE 6.3.7**, from left: lining, batting, lower piece, and two upper pieces), place the main and contrasting fabric on top of each other with right sides together and pin in place (**FIGURE 6.3.8**). Sew at ⅜ in from the raw edge and repeat on the other side (**FIGURE 6.3.9**). Iron press to open the seams (**FIGURE 6.3.10**).

FIGURE 6.3.7

FIGURE 6.3.8

FIGURE 6.3.9

FIGURE 6.3.10 *See the difference pressing makes! The right side is flat and crisp while the left side remains unpolished.*

Step 4: Adding a Neat Finish to the Zipper

Cut a tiny piece of fabric (you could even use scrap fabric) to cover both endings of the zipper, making sure it is wide enough to have a bit of overhang on each side (**FIGURE 6.3.11A**). Fold the raw edges under to hide them inside (**FIGURE 6.3.11B**).

Secure with pins and sew close to the edge (**FIGURE 6.3.11C**). Repeat with the other side (**FIGURE 6.3.11D**).

TIP This step won't be visible, it will remain hidden on the inside, but for me is almost essential to keep the zipper aligned and firm, even if I open it to maneuver at the machine.

TIP Sew as close as you can to the edge next to the zipper (see the dotted line in **FIGURE 6.3.11C**). Open the zipper so the pulling tab doesn't get in the way under the presser foot.

FIGURE 6.3.11A

FIGURE 6.3.11B

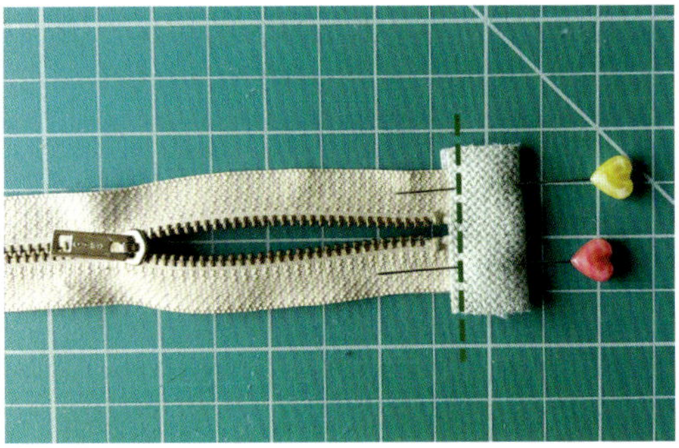

FIGURE 6.3.11C

FIGURE 6.3.11D

Step 5: Quilting

If you are not adding the quilt effect, skip to the next step.

Place the batting on top of the main fabrics you previously joined, wrong sides together, and pin in place (**FIGURE 6.3.12**). You'll notice the batting is ⅜ in smaller than the main fabrics. Draw your desired quilting design on the batting (**FIGURE 6.3.13A–B**).

TIP I suggest you start with a simple line design to practice your straight lines before trying a more intricate one.

FIGURE 6.3.13A

FIGURE 6.3.12

FIGURE 6.3.13B

Once the design is finished, you can sew all layers together following the lines by placing it on the machine with the drawn lines facing up. It is very important to sew right up to the very edge of the fabric and not only the batting (**FIGURE 6.3.14**). This way the start of all these stitch lines will be hidden on the inside of the seams, preventing it from unstitching.

TIP Sew around the entire piece first. The orange dotted line would be next on my sewing order (**FIGURE 6.3.15**). This prevents the batting from shifting shape or distorting.

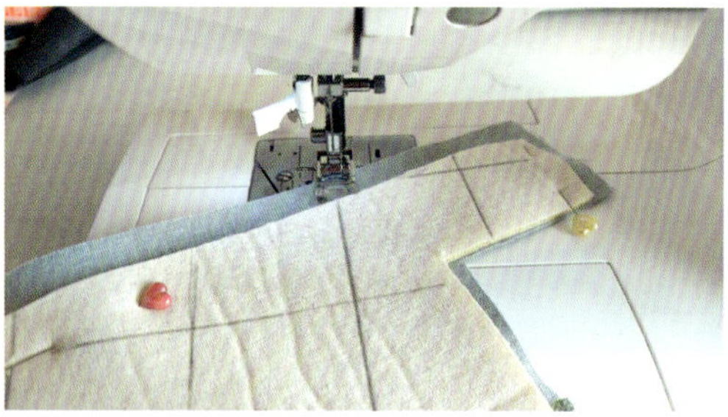

FIGURE 6.3.14

FIGURE 6.3.15

FIGURE 6.3.16 *How the pouch will look with the quilting done*

Step 6: Attaching the Zipper to the Pouch

Place the zipper on top of the quilted main piece, right sides together (**FIGURE 6.3.17**). (The right side of the zipper is where the pulling tab is facing up). Top with the lining fabric, wrong side facing up. Pin in place making sure all raw edges align and that the zipper is sandwiched between the two fabrics firmly (**FIGURE 6.3.18**).

> **TIP** The zipper's ends we stitched earlier are supposed to have a bit of overhang so they remain hidden; in case you want them to be visible, just make sure the zipper ends match the edge of the pattern when you are adjusting the width.

To sew at the machine, change your regular presser foot for the zipper foot (**FIGURE 6.3.19**). This type of presser foot has space on either side so the zipper teeth can pass through the machine freely toward the back. The needle will land next to the zipper teeth.

FIGURE 6.3.17

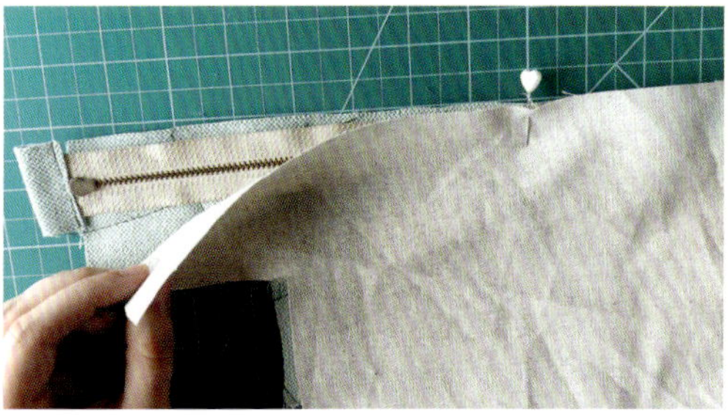

FIGURE 6.3.18

FIGURE 6.3.19

TIP I like to start my stitches about 1 inch from the pulling tab with the zipper fully closed (**FIGURE 6.3.20**). Starting with the secret sauce is crucial at this point. Stitch the entire zipper up to the opposite end, back tack, and remove from the machine cutting the extra threads. Afterward, to sew the remaining bit we left open near the pulling tab, all you need to do is open the zipper entirely to keep it out of the way (**FIGURE 6.3.21**), then sew to close as usual.

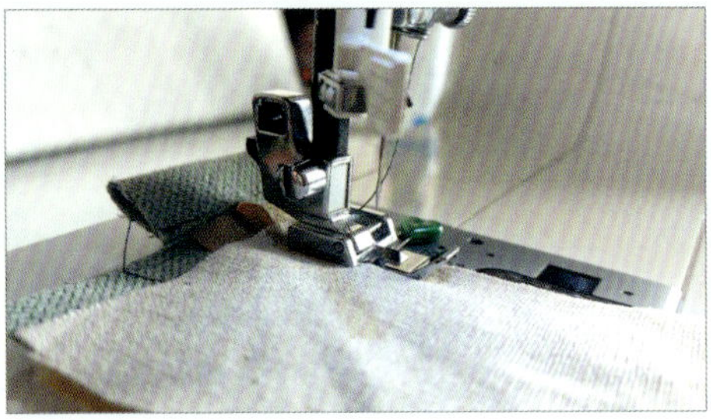

FIGURE 6.3.20

FIGURE 6.3.21

Step 7: Sewing the Other Side

"Open" the piece by pulling the lining to the right side, exposing the zipper teeth (**FIGURE 6.3.22**).

Match the "free" quilted side to the zipper, right sides together, and then the remaining raw edge of the lining to the wrong side of the zipper (**FIGURE 6.3.23A–B**). Pin in place and sew the zipper the same way as in the previous step.

FIGURE 6.3.22

FIGURE 6.3.23A

FIGURE 6.3.23B

Now that you are opening the zipper to finish this step, make sure it remains open throughout the rest of the steps so you are able to turn the final piece right side out.

Step 8: Closing the Openings Near the Zipper

Right now you should have a flat piece with the quilting fabric on one side and the lining on top, with the zipper sandwiched between them on the inside (**FIGURE 6.3.24**).

Get the lining out of the way and sew a line of straight stitches on either side of the zipper, joining both quilted layers. Do not sew over the zipper, you need to keep the lines separate, as their own, like the dotted orange line (**FIGURE 6.3.25**). Repeat on the other quilted side.

Do the same for the lining. Sew two separate seams with a straight stitch to join the lining opening near the zipper (**FIGURE 6.3.26A–B**).

FIGURE 6.3.24

FIGURE 6.3.25

FIGURE 6.3.26A

FIGURE 6.3.26B

Make sure the stitch is not catching anything from the quilted layer. Skip the zipper, do not sew over it. The thread knot in the picture is exactly where I back tack for each seam, so the loose threads got tangled (**FIGURE 6.3.27**).

FIGURE 6.3.27

Step 9: Closing the 90° Angles

Pinch the lining by one of its square angles and pull it open (**FIGURE 6.3.28A–B**). This will naturally join both angles into a straight line with right sides together. Pin in place and sew at the machine at ⅜ in, remembering to use the secret sauce (**FIGURE 6.3.29**).

FIGURE 6.3.28A

FIGURE 6.3.28B

FIGURE 6.3.29

Repeat with the quilted layer, closing the square angles the same way as with the lining; the zipper pouch has four of these openings on the quilted side, and another four on the lining side.

TIP Since this seam starts on a diagonal, focus on starting it right behind the fabric, even if that means doing your first manual stitch on the air. This will ensure that the entire opening is closed without any surprise holes. The same applies at the opposite end (**FIGURE 6.3.30A–B**).

FIGURE 6.3.30A

FIGURE 6.3.30B

Once all are sewn, you'll have a three-dimensional product. The squared angle seams are the vertical seams on either side of the zipper tab. Turn the entire piece right side out through the opening we cut earlier on the lining (**FIGURE 6.3.31A–C**).

FIGURE 6.3.31A

FIGURE 6.3.31B

FIGURE 6.3.31C

Step 10: Closing the Inner Lining Opening

Pull the opening outside. Finger press the raw edge inside about ¼ in (**FIGURE 6.3.32**). Hold it in place with sewing pins (**FIGURE 6.3.33**). Just like the topstitch used to enclose the raw edge at the placemat set, stitch a straight line, firmly back tacking at the beginning and end to close it (**FIGURE 6.3.34**). When sewn with matching thread, this looks seamless.

FIGURE 6.3.32

FIGURE 6.3.33

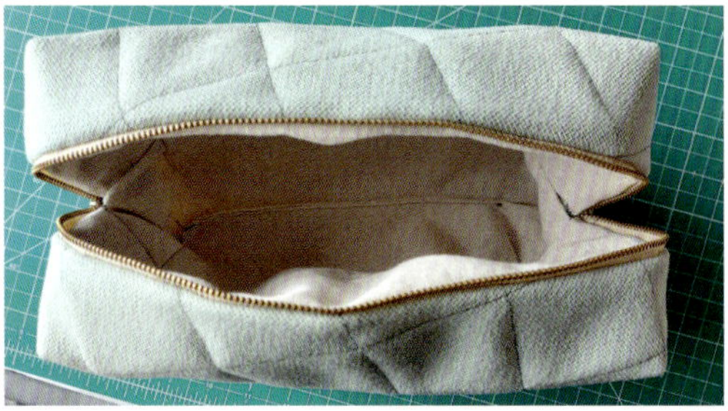

FIGURE 6.3.34

FIGURE 6.3.35
The final product!

PROJECT 4 UTILITARIAN APRON

This apron is fully customizable if you dare to play with self-drafted pockets, color combos, lengths, and fabrics. Again, we are finishing an entire project with only a sewing machine, counting on finishings like facings, overcast stitching, and enclosed raw edges.

This utilitarian apron brings you one step closer to creating your own clothes, being the first wearable project of the book.

WHAT YOU'LL NEED

- Base supplies (see page 96)
- PDF sewing pattern (Download at rockynook.com/sewing_patterns)
- Main fabric A (I am using beige canvas): 1 yd, 59 in (150 cm) wide
- Contrast fabric B (I am using brown canvas): ½ yd, 59 in (150 cm) wide
- Matching polyester thread (I will sew with a contrasting thread so it is more visible for you, but this also brings a nice topstitch quality to the finished piece if you wish to try it.)

FABRIC SUGGESTIONS

Choose a medium/heavy-weight woven fabric that presses very well, like canvas, gabardine, poplin, or linen. It's better in this situation to refrain from stretchy materials.

CUTTING LIST

For this project you need to have:

- Front (piece 1)—cut 1 ON FOLD from main fabric (A)
- Facing (piece 2)—cut 1 ON FOLD from contrasting fabric (B)
- Strap (piece 3)—cut 2 ON FOLD from contrasting fabric (B)
- Strap loop (piece 4)—cut 2 from main fabric (A)
- Pocket (piece 5)—cut 1 from contrasting fabric (B)

You can choose to cut the pieces out on different fabric depending on the color combo you wish to have.

FOR ALL SEAMS Seam allowance is ⅜ in. Back tack at the beginning and end of each seam and cut all loose threads (unless a certain step says otherwise).

SKILL SET

This project will help you practice:

- Curved facings and seams
- Garment construction
- Transferring dots
- Pivoting
- Mitered corners
- Overcast stitch

TIP Transfer all indicators (such as dots and notches) from the pattern to the fabric.

For Dots: Before cutting the outer edge of the fabric, and with your pattern still on top of the fabric, pin right in the center of the dot going all the way through, piercing the fabric (**FIGURE 6.4.1**).

Lift the paper pattern, and on the right side of the fabric mark with pencil or tailor's chalk right where the pin is (**FIGURE 6.4.2A–B**). Repeat on both sides of the apron.

This will result in four dots in the upper center of the apron. In step 6, we'll match the pocket there.

FIGURE 6.4.1

FIGURE 6.4.2A

FIGURE 6.4.2B

TIP Before starting, know that this is the first pattern in the book to omit the double colored line representing the seam allowance. This is for you to get familiar with only seeing the final cutting line, as all commercial sewing patterns show. Additionally, if you wish to have a wider apron you can adjust using the "lengthen - shorten here" line. If you wish to add length you can simply make the bottom longer because it falls straight.

Step 1: Iron Press

With all fabric pieces ready (**FIGURE 6.4.3**), begin by pressing the following (the pressing will lead to a folded finishing to keep them from unraveling after lots of wear and washes):

- Front (piece 1) lengthwise ⅜ in toward the wrong side (only the straight sides, not the armhole curve)
- 2 Straps (piece 3) lengthwise ⅜ in toward the wrong side
- 2 Strap loops (piece 4) lengthwise ⅜ in toward the wrong side
- Pocket (piece 5) all raw edges at ⅜ in toward the wrong side

With raw edges ready on all pieces, fold the straps and strap loops in half lengthwise. The pocket is ready to be topstitched as is. The front side seam will remain pressed and unstitched for a few more steps.

FIGURE 6.4.3

TIP With the help of a ruler, trace a line that is double the amount needed to create that folded edge (**FIGURE 6.4.4A**). For instance, these pieces need to have a ⅜-in fold, so trace the line at ¾ in from the raw edge and align said raw edge to the newly traced line (**FIGURE 6.4.4B**). This ensures the entire fold is even at the desired width through the entire length (**FIGURE 6.4.4C**).

FIGURE 6.4.4A

FIGURE 6.4.4B

FIGURE 6.4.4C

In the case of both straps, only one end will be finished (the other remains raw). Press the corners toward the wrong side **(FIGURE 6.4.5A)**, then fold the raw edge in the same direction (**FIGURE 6.4.5B**). Again, fold in half lengthwise (**FIGURE 6.4.5C**). This encloses the opening and creates a flatter surface to topstitch and close (**FIGURE 6.4.5D**).

To keep all this pressing in place, topstitch as close to the edge as you can, as follows:

- 2 Strap loops (piece 4): lengthwise, leaving both narrow ends raw (**FIGURE 6.4.5E**)
- 2 Straps (piece 3): lengthwise, pivoting toward the folded opening (**FIGURE 6.4.5F)**
- Pocket (piece 5): all edges by pivoting (**FIGURE 6.4.5G**)

FIGURE 6.4.5A

FIGURE 6.4.5B

FIGURE 6.4.5C

FIGURE 6.4.5D

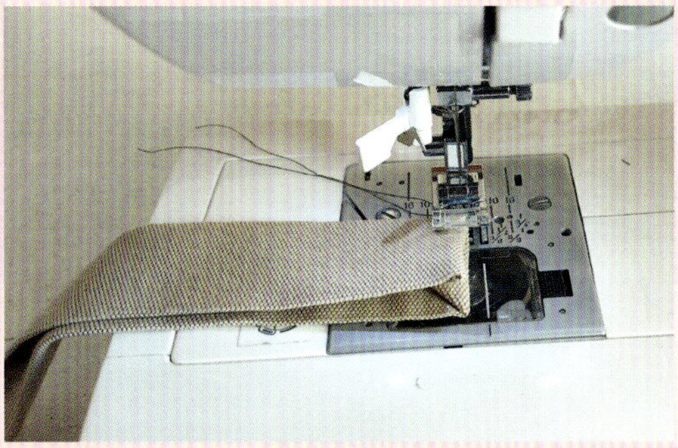

FIGURE 6.4.5E

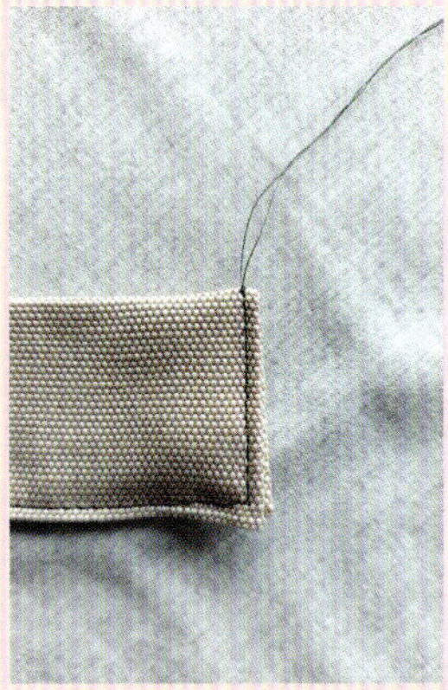

FIGURE 6.4.5F

FIGURE 6.4.5G

Step 2: Overcasting the Facing

To preserve the inner raw edge of the facing (**FIGURE 6.4.6**) (which won't be enclosed but visible) you could choose another finishing like Hong Kong seams, bias tape, folding, or even an overlock seam (if you have that additional machine). In case you want a similar finish to the overlock and you've only got your trustworthy regular machine, a similar stitch can be sewn, called an overcast stitch. It creates a sort of closed-loop zigzag stitch. (Look for it in your machine's manual—in mine it corresponds to stitch 20 (**FIGURE 6.4.7**).) To mimic this manually, sew with a zigzag stitch and do a second passing of straight stitching next to it to create a similar finish.

FIGURE 6.4.6

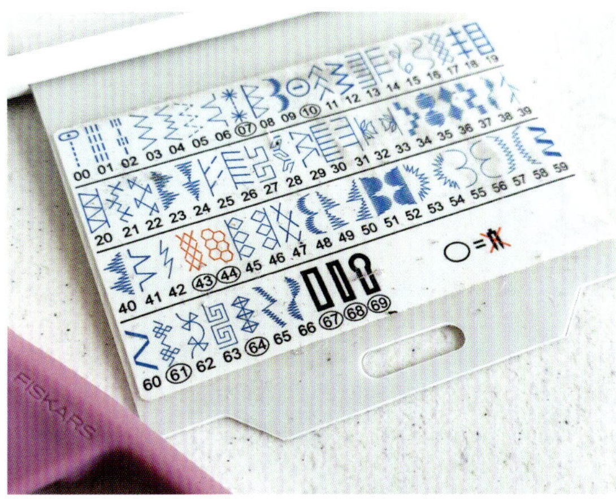

FIGURE 6.4.7

At the sewing machine you can sew this stitch with your usual presser foot (**FIGURE 6.4.8**). Pivot to create an uninterrupted stitch, especially with this type of intricate stitching (**FIGURE 6.4.9**).

FIGURE 6.4.8

> **TIP** Make a few samples every time you try a new stitch before sewing your actual garment pieces. I am keeping a ⅜-inch distance from the raw edge to the needle, but you could stitch closer to the edge if that's your preference. We will cut the excess fabric anyway.

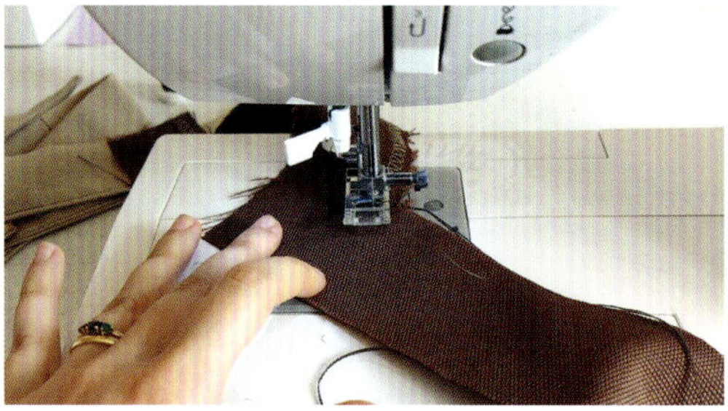

FIGURE 6.4.9

Optional: I like doing a second passing of a regular straight stitch at the edge of the overcast to further secure the finishing before trimming the excess seam allowance (**FIGURES 6.4.10A–C**).

FIGURES 6.4.10A

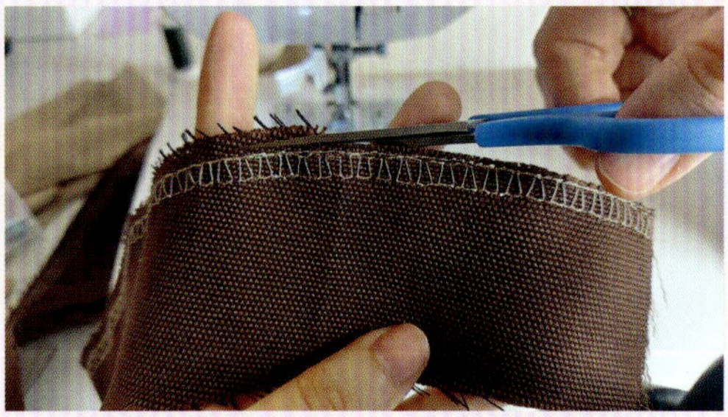

FIGURES 6.4.10B

FIGURES 6.4.10C

FIGURE 6.4.11

Step 3: Assembling the Apron

After all the pressing and finishing prep-work, we can assemble almost the entire apron to sew. Place the front piece right side facing up. On top, place the straps on each side, aligning the raw edges and matching the outer side of the straps (where the topstitch is) with its corresponding notch (here, signaled by yellow pins, at ⅝ in from the armhole raw edge) (**FIGURE 6.4.11**). Pin both straps in place to the front piece (**FIGURE 6.4.12**).

Right sides together, add the facing on top to sandwich the straps between front and facing (**FIGURE 6.4.13**). Align all raw edges. Pin in place.

FIGURE 6.4.12

FIGURE 6.4.13

Near the folded side seam, you'll notice the facing is shorter and won't reach the side's raw edge, this is correct. Fold the strap loops in half and sandwich them between front and facing (**FIGURE 6.4.14**). Each side needs a loop.

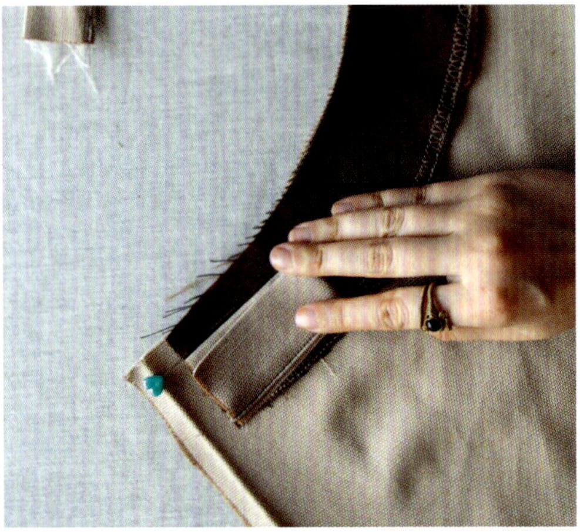

FIGURE 6.4.14

TIP To position correctly, align the loop's raw edges to the facing raw edge, and place it ⅜ inch below the curved raw edge. In the picture you can see the correct positioning of the loop—just remember you need to sandwich it between the front and facing (**FIGURE 6.4.15**).

FIGURE. 6.4.15

Step 4: Trimming the Edges

Pin all layers together (**FIGURE 6.4.16**). Sew with straight stitch at ⅜ in from side to side, pivoting at the corners near the straps. Sew another straight line parallel to the facing's raw edge to secure the strap loops (**FIGURE 6.4.17**).

Cut the excess fabric on the outer edge from the squared angle created by these seams (**FIGURE 6.4.18**). Then, grade the facing's seam allowance, careful not to cut over the seam. Trim the top corner (**FIGURE 6.4.19**) and clip the curved seam allowance (**FIGURE 6.4.20**).

FIGURE 6.4.16

FIGURE 6.4.17

FIGURE 6.4.18

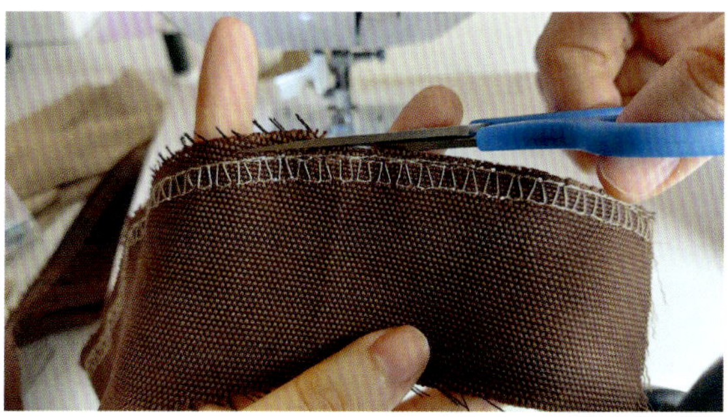

FIGURE 6.4.19

FIGURE 6.4.20

Step 5: Mitered Corners

Turn the entire apron right side out. Thanks to the trimmed excess fabric, all corners and seams are crisp and neat. As with the place-mat, poke the seams with a pointed tool to get them right on the edge (**FIGURE 6.4.21**). The folded side seam should naturally fold for another inch, leaving the previously folded ⅜ in under.

FIGURE 6.4.21

Measure the width of the fold throughout the entire garment to make sure it is consistent (**FIGURE 6.4.22**). Give the top, armholes, and side seams a good press with a hot iron.

For the bottom raw edge, iron as you did with the sides, firstly at ⅜ in toward the wrong side, and again at 1 in, folding over so the raw edge remains hidden inside (**FIGURE 6.4.23**). Open the pressed corners to reveal the grid that will guide us in sewing the mitered corners.

Sewing the mitered corners: Draw a diagonal line at the corner that passes right through the first intersection of lines (**FIGURE 6.4.24**). Fold it right sides together and do a line of straight stitches following the pencil line starting from the intersection (**FIGURE 2.4.25A–B**). It is very important to catch this entire fold, trying not to fall short. Back tack, then finish the stitch before reaching the folded raw edge (on my left). Trim the excess fabric on top (**FIGURE 2.4.26**).

FIGURE 6.4.22

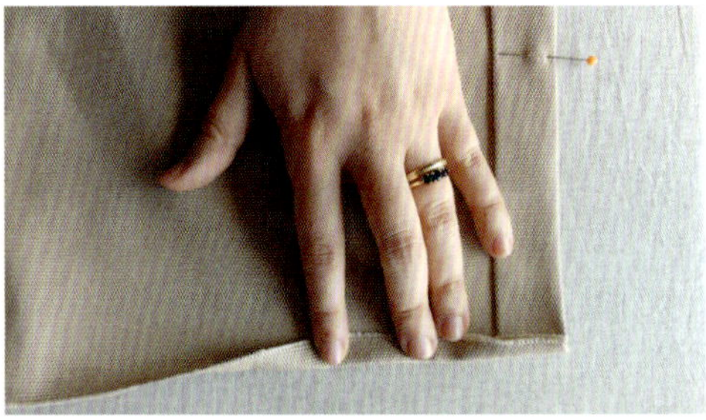

FIGURE 6.4.23

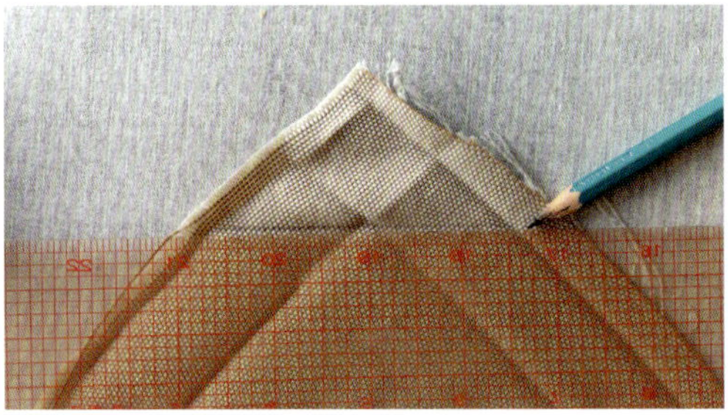

FIGURE 6.4.24

FIGURE 6.4.25A

FIGURE 6.4.25B

FIGURE 6.4.26

Turn it inside out to reveal a secured mitered corner. Pin in place (**FIGURE 6.4.27**) to topstitch around the entire apron as close to the FOLDED edge as possible, as we've done for the previous exercises (**FIGURE 6.4.28**). The topstitch goes through the top, both armholes, both sides, and bottom by pivoting.

TIP I like to start from the facing so the heavier stitch from the back tack isn't as visible.

FIGURE 6.4.27

FIGURE 6.4.28

Step 6: Pockets

With the pocket ready (with all sides topstitched and finished), lay it on top of the apron, matching each corner to the dots you marked earlier while cutting the fabric (**FIGURE 6.4.29**).

Pin in place to sew at the machine as close to the edge as you can (**FIGURE 6.4.30**). This will result in a double topstitch look from the right side. Sew the sides and bottom leaving an opening at the top. Back tack at the beginning and end and pivot to sew the square without interrupting the stitches.

FIGURE 6.4.29

FIGURE 6.4.30

FIGURE 6.4.31 *The final product!*

PROJECT 5 PAJAMA SET

This project is a super comfy two-piece set for lounging or sleeping that puts into practice all the sewing knowledge gathered so far to create a wearable outfit. You'll be surprised at how easy and quick the construction and sewing of these two garments is—perfect to kickstart your me-made wardrobe! The PJ set consists of woven shorts with an elastic waist and a stretchy t-shirt finished with a double needle.

WHAT YOU'LL NEED

- Base supplies (see page 96)
- PDF sewing pattern (Download at rockynook.com/sewing_patterns)
- Main fabric A for the top (I am using a combination of two jersey fabrics): 1 yd, 59 in (150 cm) wide
- Main fabric B for the shorts (I am using beige linen): 1 yd, 59 in (150 cm) wide
- Elastic: ½ in wide (length determined by your own waist circumference)
- 2 Safety pins
- Twin needle (optional)
- Matching polyester thread (I will sew with a contrasting thread so it is more visible for you, but this also brings a nice topstitch quality to the finished piece if you wish to try it.)

FABRIC SUGGESTIONS

Top: Choose a lightweight stretchy fabric (40%–50% stretch) like jersey, rib knit, or gauze.

Shorts: Choose a medium/lightweight woven fabric that presses very well, like linen, or poplin—or you could even try it with matching stretch fabric from the top.

You can choose to cut the pieces on different fabrics depending on the color combo you wish to have.

FOR ALL SEAMS Seam allowance is ⅜ inch. Back tack at the beginning and end of each seam and cut all loose threads (unless a certain step says otherwise).

CUTTING LIST

For this project you need to have:

- Top front (piece 1)—cut 1 ON FOLD from main fabric (A)
- Top back (piece 2)—cut 1 ON FOLD from main fabric (A)
- Top neck binding (piece 3)—cut 1 from main fabric (A)
- Top sleeves (piece 4)—cut 2 from main fabric (A)
- Shorts front (piece 1)—cut 2 from main fabric (B)
- Shorts back (piece 2)—cut 2 from main fabric (B)

SKILL SET

This project will help you practice:

- Sewing a zigzag stitch (for stretch)
- Using a twin needle
- Using notches
- Setting a sleeve
- Adding elastic
- Overcast stitch

TIP Begin with all your pieces cut. Notches on the pattern are crucial for this project, so make sure you transfer them from the pattern to the wrong side of your fabric. You can either make tiny snips (shorter than ⅜ inch) or leave them traced (**FIGURE 6.5.1**).

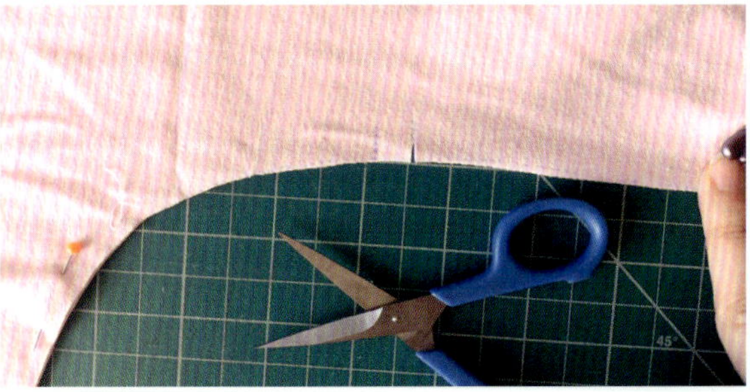

FIGURE 6.5.1

Step 1: Joining the Shoulder Seam

Start by joining together the front and back top pieces, right sides together, by one of the shoulders. Pin in place and sew with a straight stitch at ⅜ in on the machine (**FIGURE 6.5.2**). Remember to start with the secret sauce. You'll notice the frontal neckline (my sage green piece) sits lower than the back neckline (my beige piece) (**FIGURE 6.5.3**). This is correct and it's how you can identify them.

FIGURE 6.5.2

FIGURE 6.5.3

Step 2: Neck Binding

Fold the neck binding (piece 3) in half lengthwise, wrong sides together, and place on top of the neckline, right sides together. Match the short edges with the shoulder that remains open and unstitched.

Pin in place. Attach the rest of the neck binding to the neckline by pinning (**FIGURE 6.5.4**). You'll need to stretch the neck binding to fit the semi-circle created by the neckline—this is correct! The neck binding is a tad shorter than the neckline to create a narrow neck finish that stretches when you pull the top over your head.

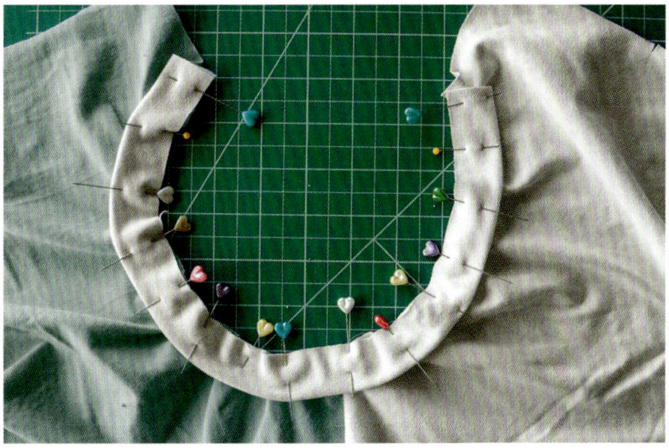

FIGURE 6.5.4

About 2 in before reaching the short edges on both sides, mark with different pins (in my case, heart-shaped head pins) to alert you that the end toward the edge will be left unstitched for now (**FIGURE 6.5.5**).

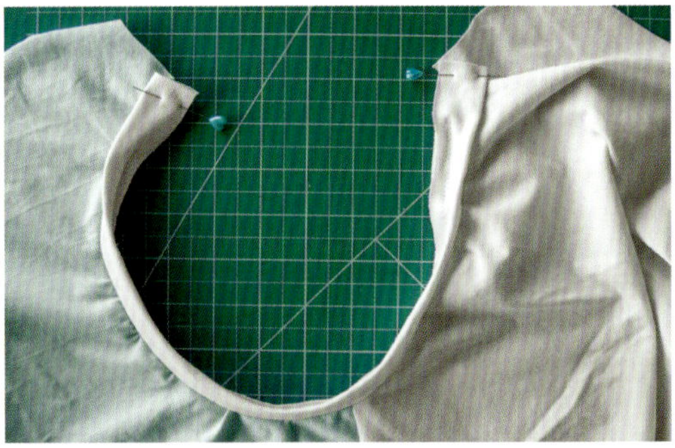

FIGURE 6.5.5

At the machine, set your stitch to zigzag. Start and finish at the markings with different pins, remembering to back tack both the beginning and end (**FIGURE 6.5.6**). You'll need to stretch the neckline and binding while sewing by pulling from the back and front gently—just to make the fabrics lie flat. You want to avoid pulling so hard that the fabric yanks to the back without the feeding dogs guiding it.

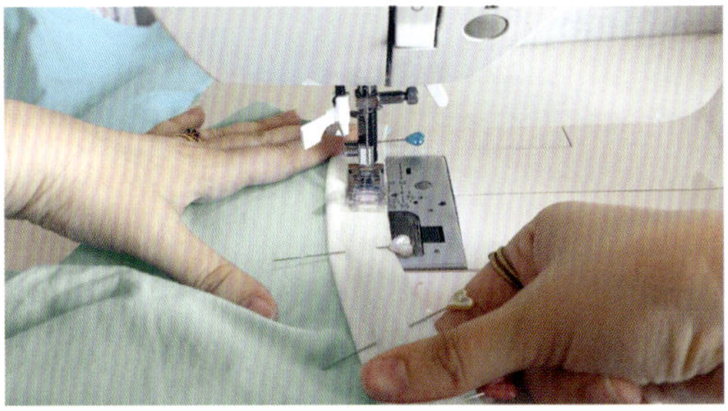

FIGURE 6.5.6

TIP I like to focus on stretching only the distance between the needle and the next sewing pin, which is usually about 2 inches. This makes it way easier, and I don't have to pull my arms too far from each other.

To close the loop, join together the remaining shoulder, right sides together, and pin in place (**FIGURE 6.5.7**). At the machine, sew a straight stitch at a ⅜-in seam allowance. The neck binding needs to match the closed shoulder we just stitched. Match the loose ends of the neck binding right sides together and pin in place (**FIGURE 6.5.8**). At the machine, sew a straight stitch at a ⅜-in seam allowance.

FIGURE 6.5.7

FIGURE 6.5.8

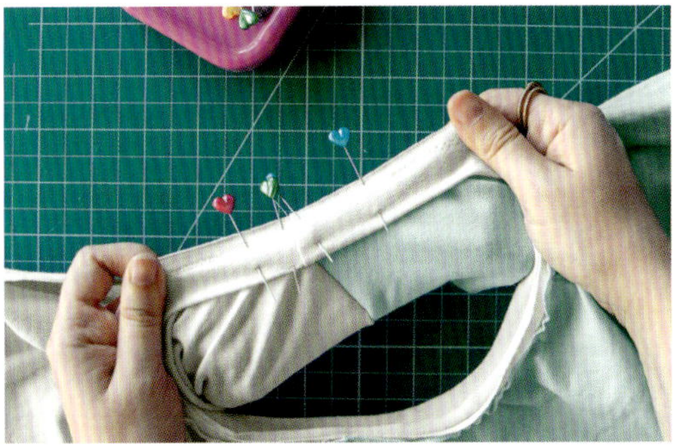

FIGURE 6.5.9

TIP I like to stretch all fabric away from the seam on either sides, in opposite directions, so the topstitch really secures the seam as flat as can be (**FIGURE 6.5.10**). This ensures the neck binding is crisp and is always in its position instead of peeking to the wrong side of the garment (**FIGURE 6.5.11**).

FIGURE 6.5.10

FIGURE 6.5.11

To finish joining together bodice to neck binding at the shoulder, sew with a zigzag stitch from where we left off. Stretch the neck binding while sewing at the machine to make the fabric lay as flat as possible. Remember to back tack the beginning and end to secure the seam (**FIGURE 6.5.9**).

With the entire neckline loop closed, topstitch the neck binding seam allowance toward the wrong side of the main bodice (away from the neck binding itself) with a zigzag stitch. Remember to start with the secret sauce and back tack at the end to match the zigzag stitches.

Step 3: Sleeves

Place the main bodice open, with right sides facing up. Next to it in the armhole, place one sleeve with the right side facing up. Make sure the sleeve corresponds to and matches that certain armhole; you can tell by the notches: double notches for the back and a single notch for the front (**FIGURE 6.5.12**).

FIGURE 6.5.12

Flip the sleeve on top of the bodice so the right sides are touching. Match each sleeve notch with its corresponding notch on the armhole and pin in place (**FIGURE 6.5.13A–B**). Start with the center notch (matching the seam that joins the front and back bodice), followed by the single notch at the front bodice, then the side seam edge, and lastly filling in the rest of that armhole side with pins (**FIGURE 6.5.14**).

FIGURE 6.5.13A

FIGURE 6.5.13B

FIGURE 6.5.14

Repeat on the back bodice and the other sleeve.

TIP The joy of setting sleeves of jersey fabric is you can stretch both pieces a tiny bit to make them fit, because the curved shapes of both armhole and sleeve may need a little help to fit together.

On the sewing machine, sew with a straight stitch at a ⅜-in seam allowance, guiding the curved armhole through very gently. Sew the other sleeve, too.

Finish the seam allowance with an overcast stitch, overlock (I did mine this way for you to see this type of finish—see **FIGURE 6.5.15**), pinking shears, or zigzag stitch. In this particular case you could even leave it raw, because jersey knit won't unravel or fray like a woven material would (**FIGURE 6.5.16**).

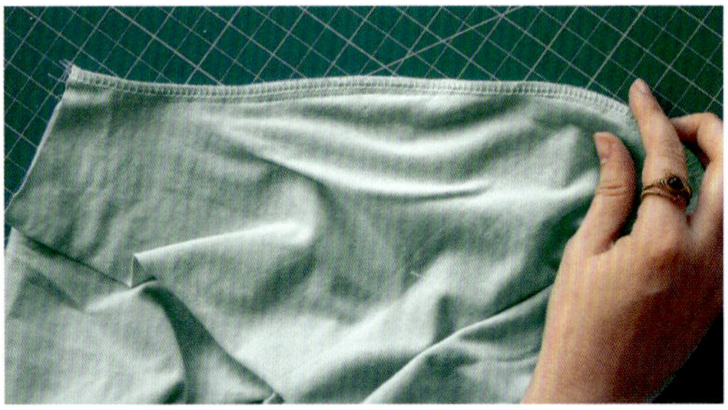

FIGURE 6.5.15

FIGURE 6.5.16

Step 4: Closing Side Seams

Join the back bodice and front bodice with right sides together, pin in place, and make sure all edges and corners match—especially the cross between the bodice and sleeve from both front and back (**FIGURE 6.5.17**). Sew the side seam with a straight stitch and ⅜-in seam allowance (**FIGURE 6.5.18**). Repeat on the other side.

TIP You might need to pivot at the armhole seam. Remember to put your needle down right at the row of stitches that connect the sleeve to the bodice.

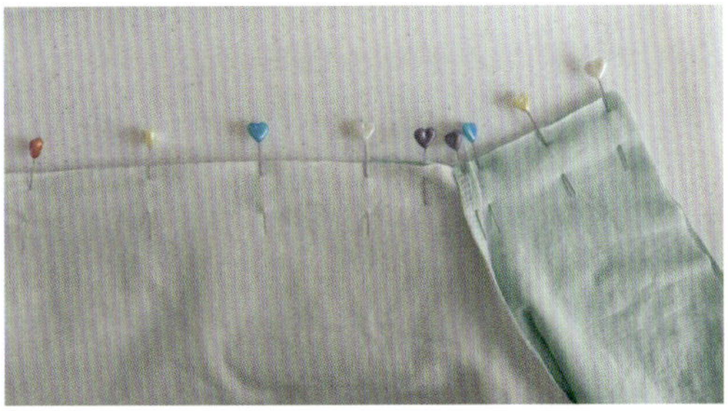

FIGURE 6.5.17

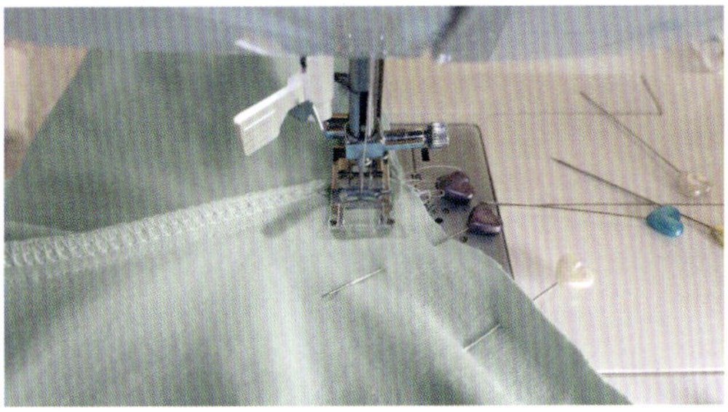

FIGURE 6.5.18

FIGURE 6.5.19 *This is how the cross between bodice (front and back) and sleeve should look from the right side, right below at the armpit.*

Step 5: Finishing Hemlines

The last step is finishing the raw edges at the bottom and the sleeves. You can either finish the raw edge with an overcast stitch, a zigzag stitch, or an overlock, or leave it raw. In my case I am using an overlock seam. To secure the hemline, fold the finished raw edge to the wrong side of the garment for ⅜ in (**FIGURE 6.5.20**). Sew with straight stitch at ⅜ in from the fold.

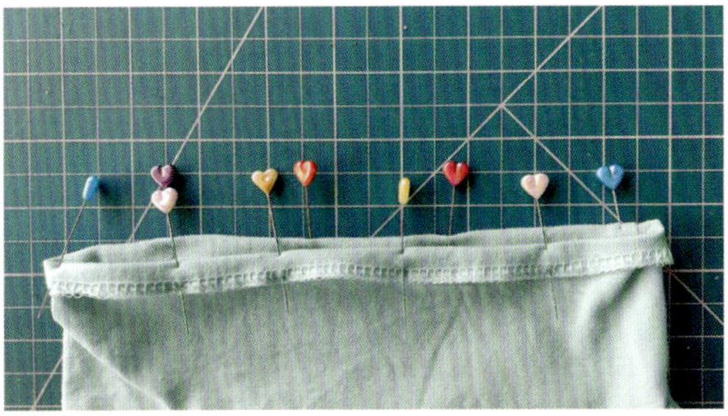

FIGURE 6.5.20

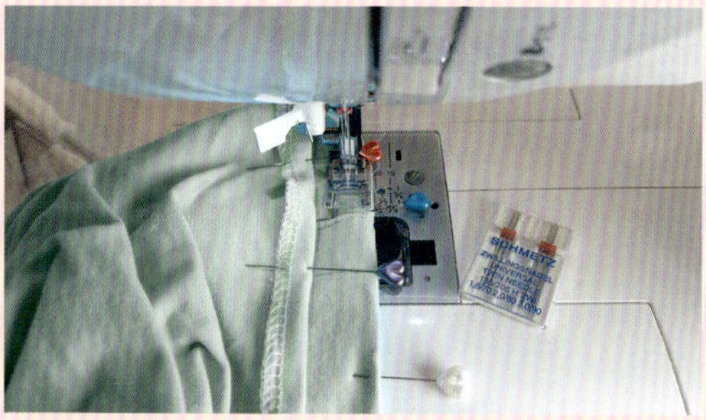

FIGURE 6.5.21

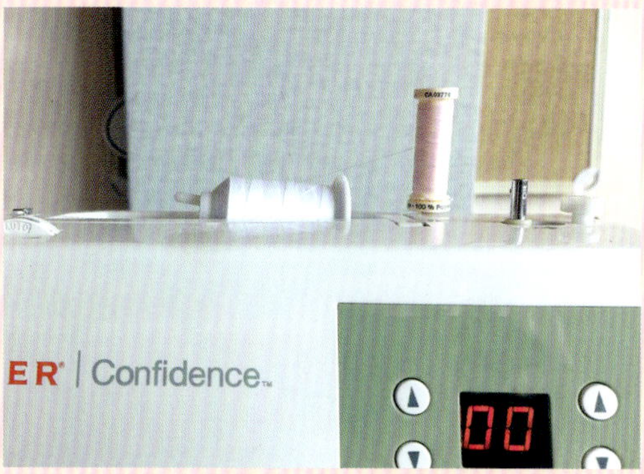

FIGURE 6.5.22 *The twin needle needs two spools to feed each needle's eye. My machine has two spool pins. If yours doesn't, you might need to buy it separately.*

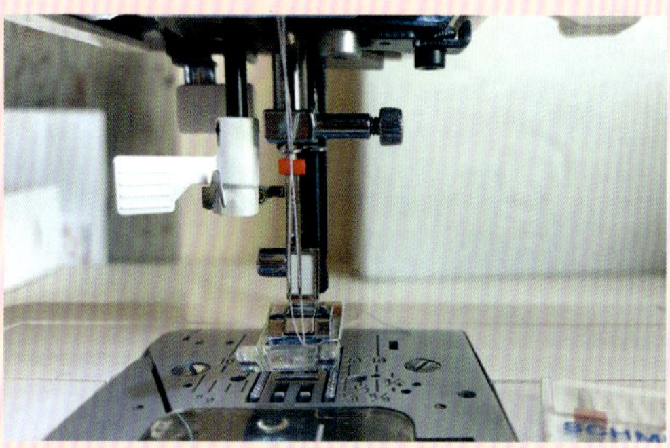

FIGURE 6.5.23 *Close up of the twin needle, with its corresponding thread in each eye. Both threads follow the regular journey from spool to needle.*

I will show you how to sew with a twin needle, but you can perfectly finish your top by sewing with regular straight stitch.

Twin Needles: The width between the needles is up to you. I have a three-pack, but you can also find them individually. Change your regular needle for the twin needle (**FIGURE 6.5.21**).

The main thing to keep in mind when using twin needles is that the garment *must* be right side facing up; otherwise, the parallel stitch-line effect would end up on the wrong side (**FIGURE 6.5.25**). (The wrong side has a zigzag look, not the parallel lines).

FIGURE 6.5.24 *Check your manual if there is anything to add so the machine knows you've inserted a twin needle. In my case there's this twin needle button I need to push. With this function enabled, if I were to adjust the needle position, the machine can warn if it would crash with the presser foot.*

FIGURE 6.5.25

Step 6: The Shorts

From the four pieces needed for the shorts, take one front (piece 1) and one back (piece 2) and place them right sides together (the front on top).

Match together the side seams and the inseams. Pin them together to secure and sew at the machine with a straight stitch at ⅜ in.

Finish all raw edges. I used an overcast stitch with a contrasting thread (**FIGURE 6.5.27**), but you could use matching thread or another type of finish. (For this woven garment, I do not recommend leaving the edges raw). Repeat with the other side, making sure that the pieces mirror each other, this ensures you'll have one correct side for each leg (**FIGURE 6.5.28**).

TIP When sewing any bottom garment (shorts, trousers, leggings) you'll notice the back piece is usually bigger than the front (**FIGURE 6.5.26**). This is to leave room for the buttocks. In this pattern, the back piece is taller at the waist and longer at the crotch.

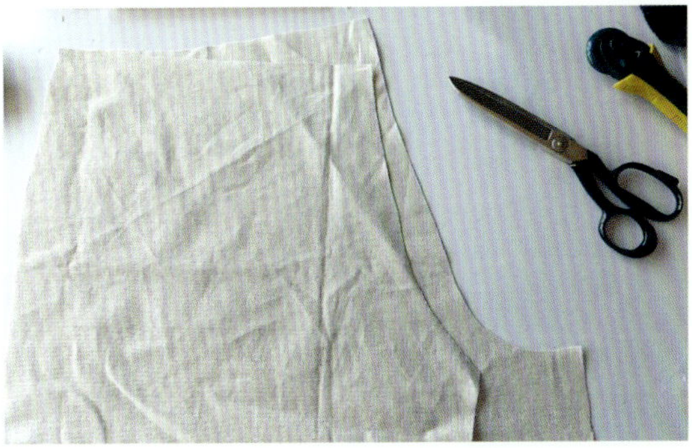

FIGURE 6.5.26

FIGURE 6.5.27

FIGURE 6.5.28

Step 7: Joining the Legs Together

Press the seam allowance of the side seams and the inseam with a hot iron toward the back (**FIGURE 6.5.29**). Then, turn *only* one leg right side out (**FIGURE 6.5.30**). This leg will go *inside* the other that still has its wrong side facing out (**FIGURE 6.5.31**).

Match the side seam from one leg with the other, then one inseam with the other, right sides together, and pin (**FIGURE 6.5.32**).

FIGURE 6.5.29

FIGURE 6.5.30

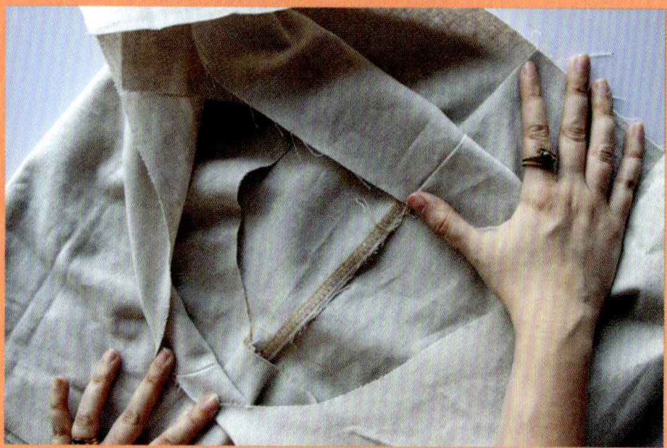

FIGURE 6.5.31

FIGURE 6.5.32

FIGURE 6.5.33

Pin together the entire curve (**FIGURE 6.5.33**). You will sew with a straight stitch at ⅜ in, starting with the holy secret sauce. Careful with the bulk generated by the seam allowances at the inseam (**FIGURE 6.5.34**). Pull a bit from behind at the machine if you feel like the fabric needs a little help to pass through the feed dogs. Pivot at the inseam if you feel like the curve is too steep.

FIGURE 6.5.35 *This is what the inside of the inseam should look like.*

FIGURE 6.5.34

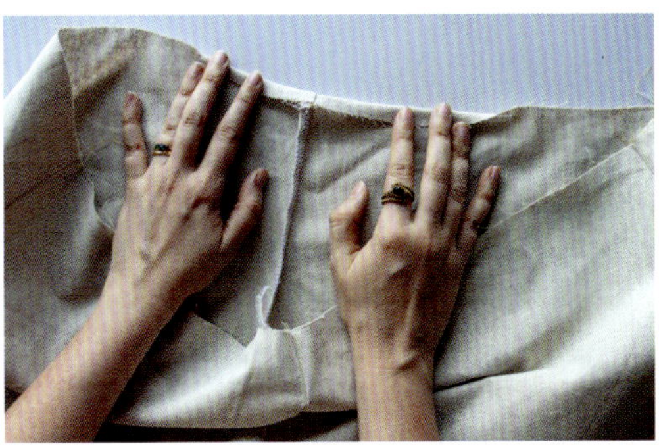

FIGURE 6.5.36

Step 8: Prep Work for the Waistline Elastic

Fold the waistline toward the wrong side for ⅜ in and then fold again 1 in, so the raw edge is hidden inside (**FIGURE 6.5.35**).

Press with a hot iron so the waistline keeps its shape (**FIGURE 6.5.37**). Pin around the entire waist leaving an 8-in opening at the center back (signaled with different sewing pins) (**FIGURE 6.5.38**). At the machine, sew with a straight stitch close to the lower edge of the fold (**FIGURE 6.5.39**). Remember the secret sauce.

FIGURE 6.5.37

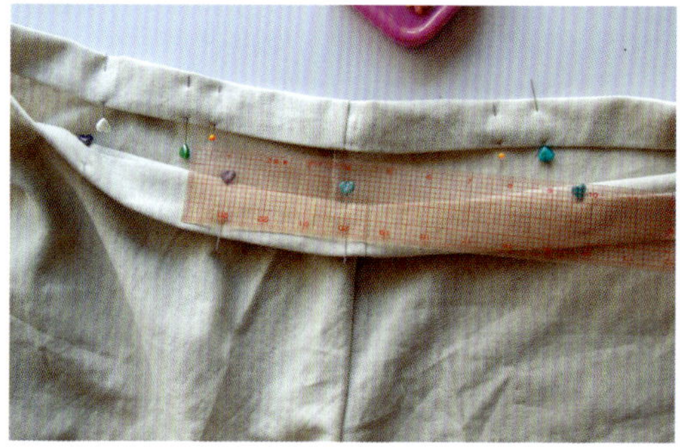

FIGURE 6.5.38

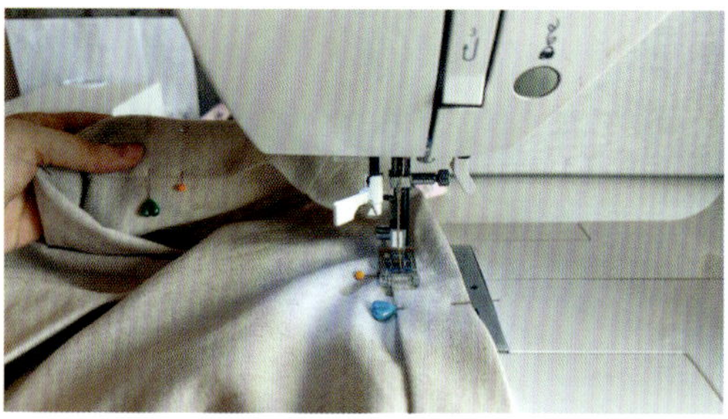

FIGURE 6.5.39

TIP In order to leave an opening, start from one pin, making sure the other one is already behind the needle. When completing the circumference, you'll reach the other pin before the one you started with.

Step 9: Measure the Elastic

Grab your elastic and measure it around your natural waist comfortably. Whatever the length, add 2 in to that and cut it (**FIGURE 6.5.40**).

TIP I like my elastics on the looser side. I'll make it a bit bigger than my waist, even before adding the 2 inches—but I've also seen sewists wrapping it around them on the tighter side, even reducing length from their circumference so it holds snugly. It's just a personal choice.

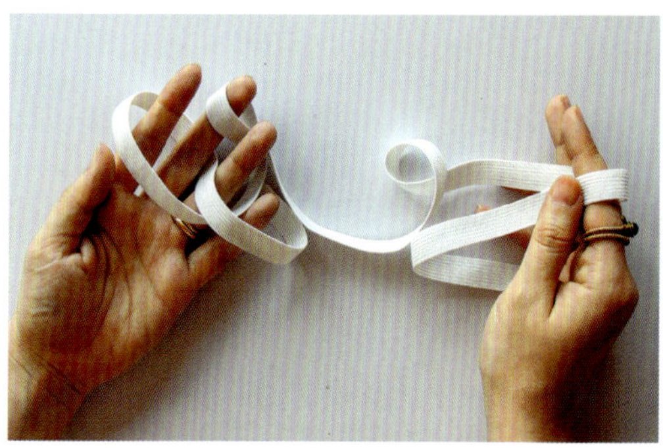

FIGURE 6.5.40

Step 10: Adding the Elastic

Put a safety pin on either end of your elastic (**FIGURE 6.5.41**). You will introduce one of them inside of the waistline fold; the other end will be secured with the safety pin to the edge of the garment (**FIGURE 6.5.42**). (This is a great tip to avoid losing the other end after putting the first end inside!)

By feeling the safety pin inside of the waistline fold, push it until you reach the opening again and it comes out. This will create natural gathers to the garment because the elastic is smaller than the overall opening of the shorts.

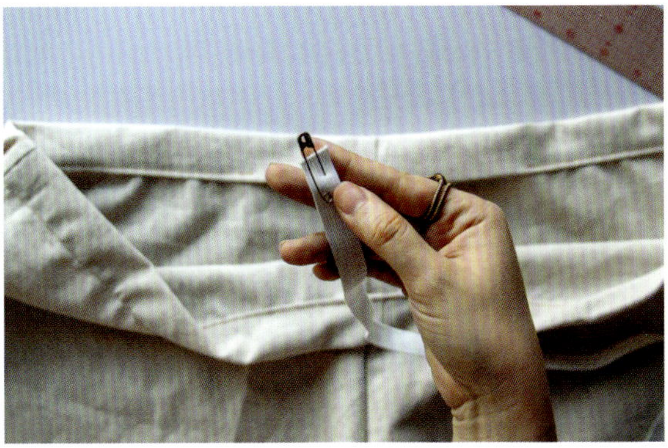

FIGURE 6.5.41

FIGURE 6.5.42

Step 11: Closing the Elastic

Overlap both ends of the elastic by 1 in and secure with pins (**FIGURE 6.5.43**). Make sure the elastic is flat, not twisted around. Sew at the machine with a straight stitch (**FIGURE 6.5.44**), creating a square by pivoting (**FIGURE 6.5.45**). Sew the stitches as close to the edge as possible.

FIGURE 6.5.43

FIGURE 6.5.44

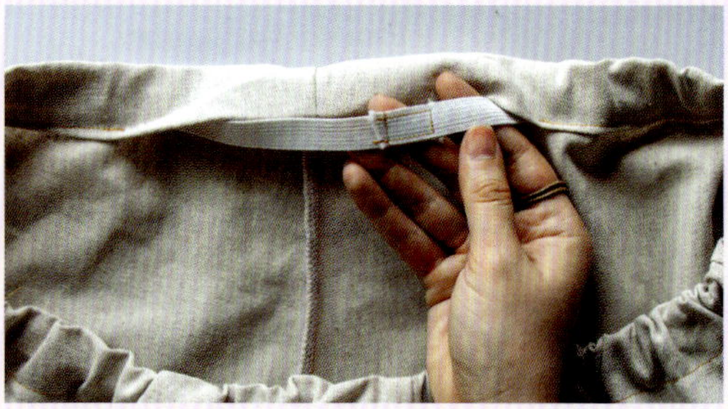

FIGURE 6.5.45

Secure the flat elastic with a pin to the center back (**FIGURE 6.5.46**). This pin will keep the elastic in place while we close the fabric opening. At the machine, close said gap using the secret sauce. Because the elastic is smaller than the waistline of the fabric, you'll need to stretch this tiny area a bit (**FIGURE 6.5.47**). Do so by holding at the front and pulling from the back gently. You only want to make it flat enough to sew straight, neat stitches; no need to pull so hard that the feeding dogs won't guide the fabric (**FIGURE 6.5.48**).

FIGURE 6.5.46

FIGURE 6.5.47

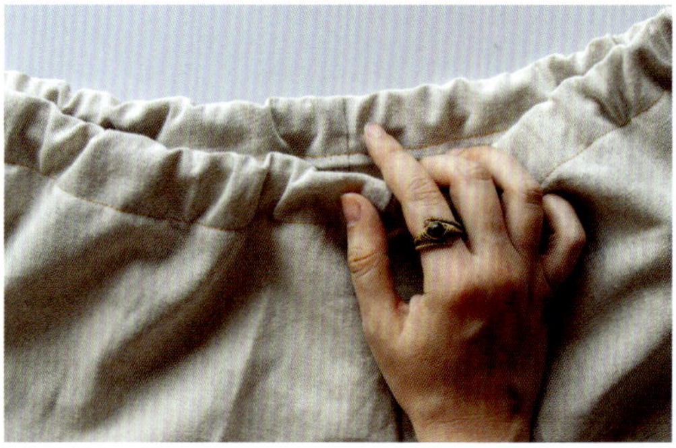

FIGURE 6.5.48 *Optional: I like to do a final "stitch in the ditch" at the center back seam to secure the elastic in its flat position. This prevents it from twisting after a few wears.*

Step 12: Finishing the Hemline

Lastly, finish the raw edge of the leg opening with your preferred method (I chose the same overcast stitch as the inseam of step 6). Fold toward the right side for ⅜ in and pin in place to then sew the bottom hemline at the sewing machine with a straight stitch.

Remember to use the secret sauce and give it a good final press.

FIGURE 6.5.49 *The final product!*

SAGE TEE AGUS
16 JUN 21
Bra Sewing Bee
Language of Bra Making - Liz Sews
cotton

CHAPTER 7

Final Tips

SEWING JOURNAL

Keeping a journal is an essential part of my sewing practice, and I encourage you to take on this practice too, especially now that you are starting to learn and dive into new information. Each entry is a project you're working on. There's no need to get fancy—simply add a scrap of the fabric you used, the name and size of the pattern, and a few annotations of the process. By keeping a record of your projects, your sewing brain will start to keep more data and you'll notice how quickly you get better and better.

These are some of the things I add to my sewing journal on each project:

1. **Name of the Project**

   Anything to identify that entry: I usually go with the commercial name of the pattern and the brand, but you could also go with the style of garment you'll be sewing, like "White Eyelet Ruffle Blouse."

2. **My Measurements**

   Yes, I measure myself each and every time I'm about to sew anything. Not only because I tend to fluctuate, but mostly because I usually fall in between sizes, so writing my measurements down next to the pattern sizing helps me to choose the correct size (**FIGURE 7.1**).

   I always include the bust, the waist, and the hip, but if a pattern requires another specific measurement like wrists or ribcage, I'll add it too.

3. **Date and Time**

   Some projects take more than a single day, (in my case most of them take about a week) because I tend to work in blocks of three to four hours in the evenings due to my working schedule. Writing exactly what I accomplished each day and how long it took gives me an accurate insight of how fast or slow I am sewing, and how challenging each project is.

   I've also come to understand that I'm not as fast when cutting and prepping the pattern versus the actual sewing. Knowing this can help me in choosing a tried-and-true pattern that is already prepared if I need to whip up a quick garment, for instance.

   Knowing how long it took you is also useful when calculating how much the final garment costs. Plus, this is the easiest way to see how much you are improving your skills (**FIGURES 7.2** and **7.3**).

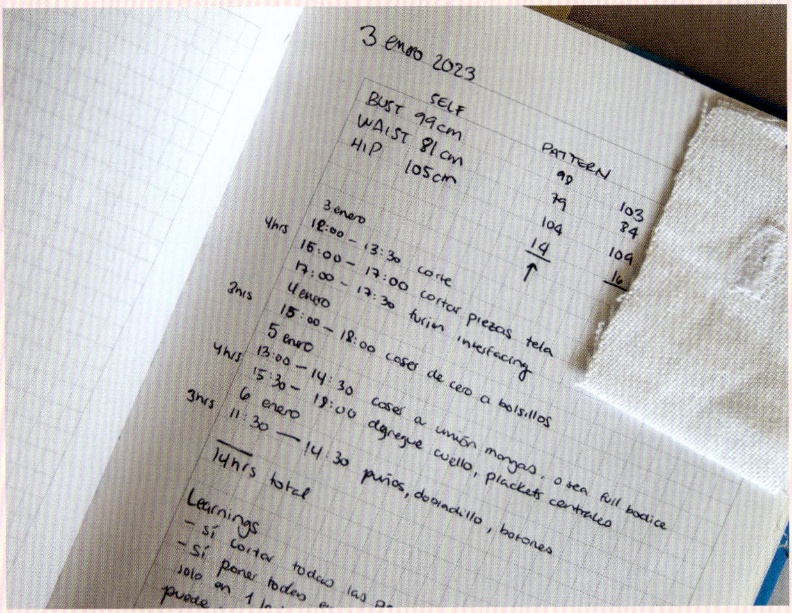

FIGURE 7.1 *Notice how I add my measurements and the pattern's in two different sizes to choose which will fit me best.*

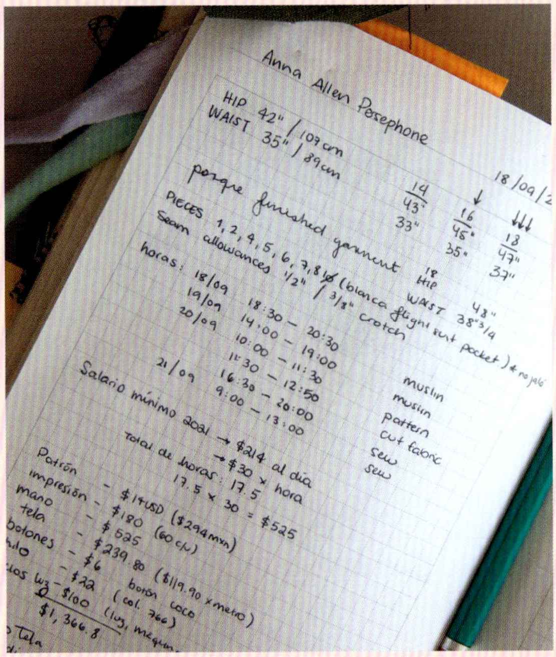

FIGURE 7.2 *Trousers that took me 17.5 hours to make*

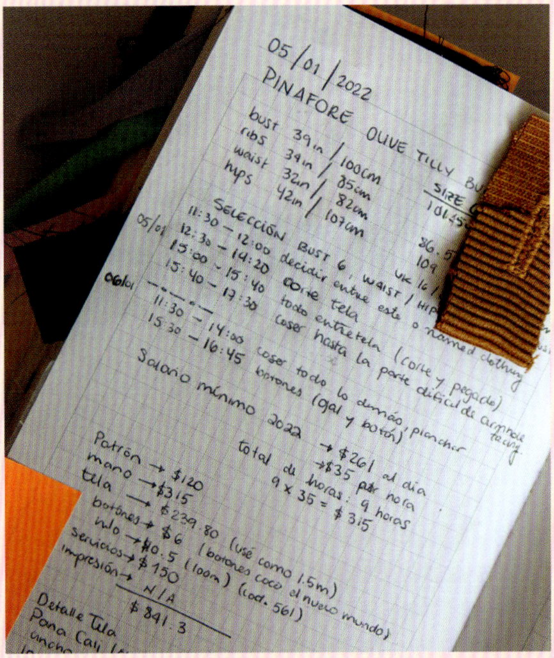

FIGURE 7.3 *A pinafore that took me 9 hours to make*

FIGURE 7.4A *I added different zigzag configurations to remember which I considered best, using the two textiles I chose to sew together for a pair of undies.*

FIGURE 7.4B *I added scraps of fabric to illustrate the overlock finish and the buttonhole size (which I used as practice). I also added a note for the overlock settings to achieve a good tension with this particular fabric.*

4. **Learning**

   This is a section to help your future self with anything you noticed while creating a project. In my sewing journal some things I include are:

   - A sizing or fit improvement I would've liked, such as choosing a different size or adding a bit of extra room to the bustline, for instance.
   - How I managed to complete an instruction I found difficult, with tips and step-by-step directions.
   - Description of a new skill I learned while sewing a challenging garment. This works great as a pat on the back from your future and past self!
   - Extra resources like video tutorials or books.
   - Things I would've done differently (in the sewing steps, or the chosen fabric, or time management notes).
   - Anything worth noting that was relevant to this particular sewing project.

5. **Fabric**

   I always add a scrap of fabric to the upper corner of my journal. If I used any additional notions or stitches I also like to add them. For example:

   - If the garment had any buttons, I'll add the scrap of fabric that I practiced the buttonholes with.
   - If it had a special lining or interfacing, I attach scraps of that along with the main fabric.
   - If I used a combination of different fabrics, I'll add them all.

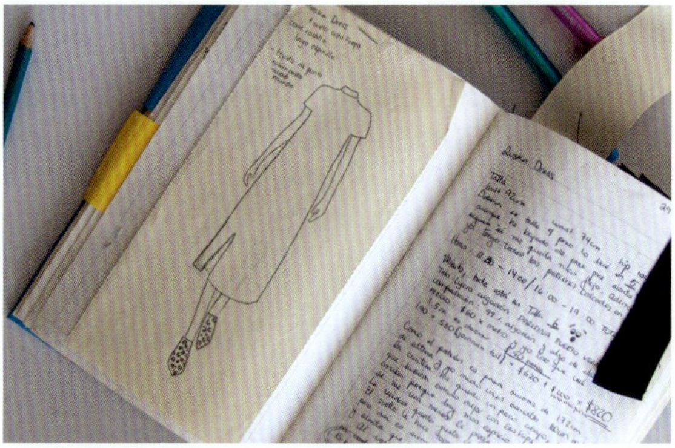

FIGURE 7.4C *Besides fabric, you can add illustrations, sketches, or other type of drawings to further explain a certain project.*

FIGURE 7.4D *I added a detailed description of how to assemble a collar stand for a button up. On the right, a scrap of fabric with the sample buttonhole.*

- If it has an overlock or an embroidery stitch, I'll add it to the scrap. You can add anything that makes it easier for you to identify that scrap to the actual garment you did (**FIGURES 7.4A–D**). Plus all the tiny colorful scraps peeking out of the pages makes an even more fun sewing journal!

6. **Costs**

   In my opinion, this section is of the utmost importance when keeping a sewing journal! Yes, we are sewing for ourselves (or maybe a loved one or two) and may not be thinking of monetizing these creations, but ever since I started calculating the cost of my garments I feel more connected to the reality of garment making and how resourceful, time-costly, and labor intensive it actually is. The resources I consider into costs are:

- Fabric: The price by the yard and how much I bought. (In my journal I include the fabric's commercial name, the composition, where I got it from, and when I got it.) This includes all fabrics used: the main fabric, the lining, the interfacing, the filling, etc.
- Sewing Pattern: The cost of the purchased pattern (and the cost of printing it, if applicable). If I sew the same pattern more than once I don't factor these into the new garment. Making another version of a garment is considerably less costly.
- Notions: Anything used to complete the garment besides fabric. This could include (but is not limited to) buttons, zippers, thread, elastics, snaps, ribbons, tassels, etc.

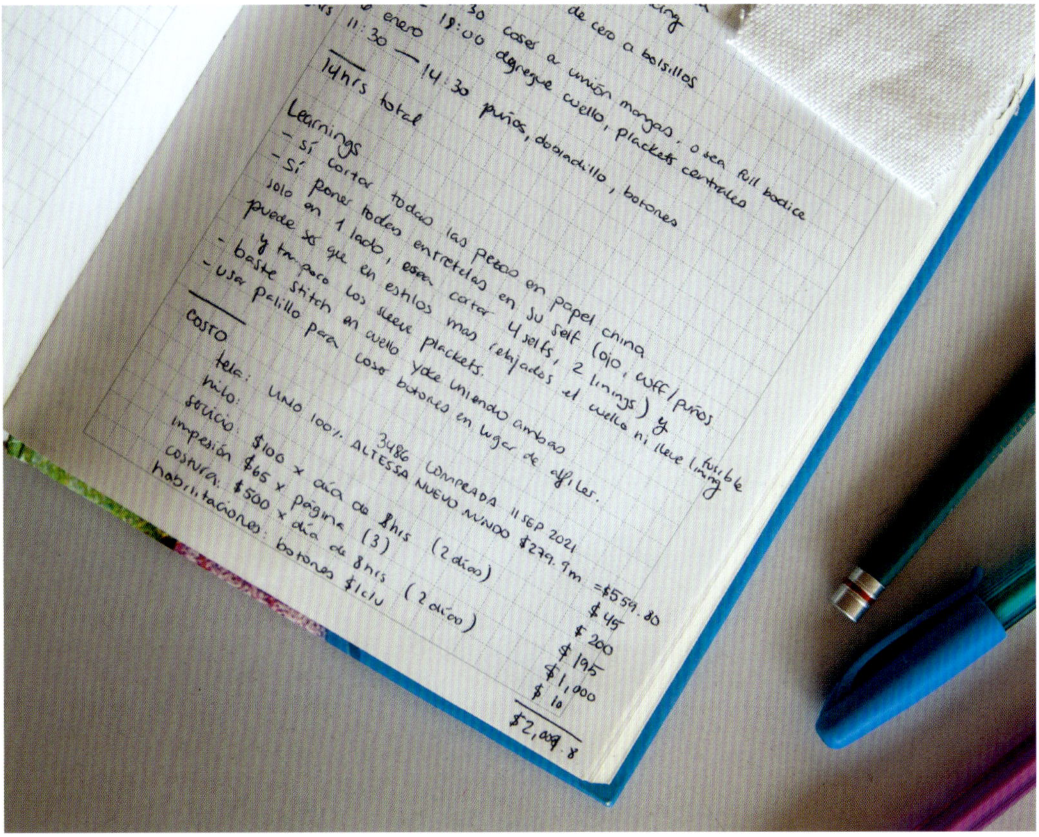

FIGURE 7.5 *The costs are at the bottom of the page, in Mexican pesos.*

- Sewing: By multiplying the hours it took to complete the garment with an hourly rate, we get the sewing cost. The hourly rate is set by you, the sewist. You can choose to guide that rate with the minimum wage of your area, the hourly rate you have in your 9 to 5, the average wage of a seamstress, or the rate of an independent designer, just to name a few options.

  The only non-negotiable is to set a rate you are comfortable with in case you do decide to monetize your creations.

- Services: This is where I include all operation costs, like electricity, Wi-Fi, or gas—in my case this is a fixed rate of $5, but it could be more or less depending on your location (**FIGURE 7.5**).

STORING PATTERNS

As I mentioned before, the print versions of all my sewing patterns are some of my most valuable possessions, so keeping them safe is crucial to my sewing practice, but there are PDF files or the traced pieces that need to be stored too, so here's a breakdown of how I do it:

PDF Files: Usually when purchasing digital sewing patterns you get more than one download. This is something most brands do to ensure you don't lose the pattern in case you change computers or need to format your hard drive or something happens to your original download. So, in addition to having multiple downloads available with the email I purchased the pattern with, I also like to keep my PDF files in my computer, an external hard drive, and the cloud. This may seem too cautious, but I currently own over 50 digital sewing patterns and losing them would be absolutely tragic. I would rather keep them in various locations to make sure I can always access them (**FIGURE 7.6**).

In the case of a PDF sewing pattern, I like to print it once and keep that as my original. When using the Copyshop file (the full-size print) that can be printed out again and again, I still only print it once (printing is oftentimes

FIGURE 7.6

costly!). I store these rolled inside my closet. A good tip is to write the name of the pattern on the outside to easily identify it without unrolling.

When using the A4/Letter format to assemble, I also only print it once because assembling takes a lot of work and time! I store these folded inside my closet. A good tip is to tape together each sheet on both sides, because sometimes the sheets overlap when folded, and that can tear the paper.

Original Print: Keeping the print safe is important when working with PDF patterns, but it is absolutely vital when you purchase a print pattern with no digital download, because that is your one and only copy. It must be protected at all costs. Usually a print pattern will come folded in its own packet along with the written instructions, so storing these small envelopes is quite easy.

Traced Pattern Pieces: I've said it before, and I'll say it again: I always retrace my pattern pieces onto tissue paper to preserve the original pattern! I keep all those retraced pattern pieces inside plastic sleeves in binders, divided by garment type. Because all pattern pieces have their information written on them, I don't need to bother labeling each plastic sleeve, but it would be nice to add some pictures or technical drawings to identify each pattern if the name isn't enough for you (**FIGURE 7.7**).

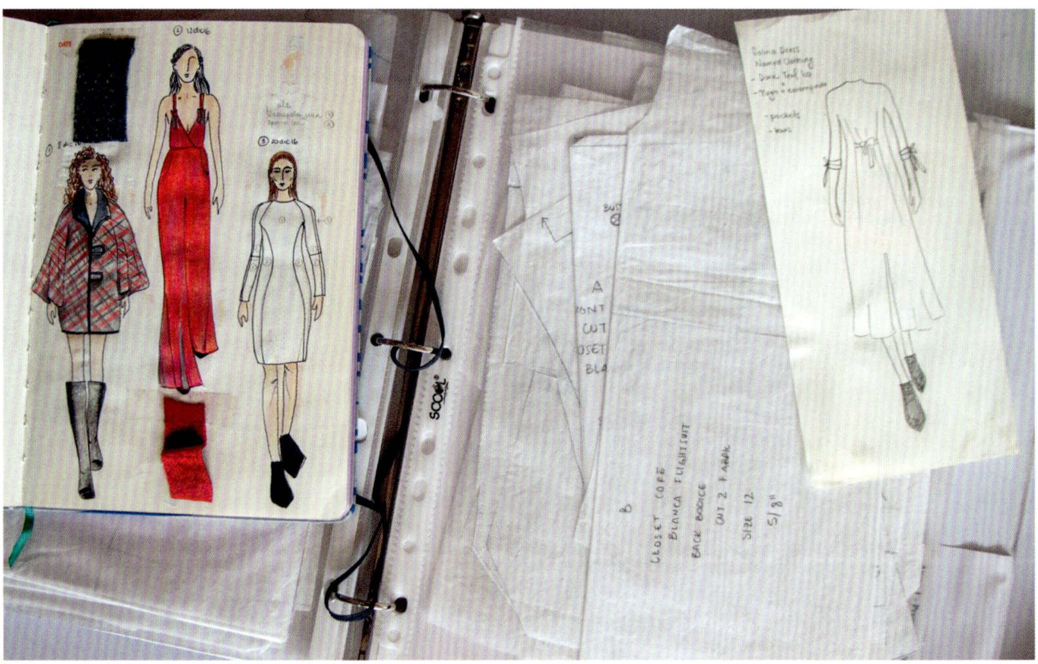

FIGURE 7.7

Whichever method you choose to store your patterns, always make sure they are labeled correctly and in a safe spot to avoid any kind of misfortune.

At the end of the day, the sewing patterns to construct a garment are as important as the garment itself.

FABRIC, PATTERNS, AND OTHER RESOURCES

- **Mood Fabrics** (moodfabrics.com)

  A supreme site to learn more about fabric, even if you don't make a purchase. Each fabric has many photos to help you truly understand the scale, the drape, and the color of the product. They also make suggestions for garments that can work with the fabric and have an additional place to download free sewing patterns.

- **Spoonflower** (spoonflower.com)

  My go-to place when looking for specific print fabric. This site excels in made-to-order prints from different artists and illustrators. You can even upload your own to create custom print garments. They work with high-quality fabrics and lots of options!

- **Garala Studio** (garalastudio.com)

  For more patterns and all info related to sewing, visit me at my website!

- **Fashionary** (fashionary.org)

  Sketchbooks, templates for human figures, and books on different fashion industry themes and fabrics.

- Don't forget to check out your local fabric, sewing, and craft stores!

ACKNOWLEDGMENTS

Firstly I would like to thank my editor Maggie Yates without whom this book would not exist. For her vision, her never ending help, for answering every single one of my questions and most importantly for trusting me with this gargantuan task.

I would also like to thank my long family line of ancestors who took sewing, woodworking, knitting, and embroidery seriously so I too could dip my toes in creative endeavors.

Another big thank you goes to anyone who has been my student on and offline, who taught me how to dissect even the most ambitious projects into the tiniest steps, so anything can be understood and accomplished with each stitch.

And last but not least, *creative women*. It never ceases to amaze me how women around me keep protecting the realm of craft and creation through their unique path, be it editing books, showing me new ways of thinking, or inspiring me to keep pursuing creativity.

PHOTOGRAPHY CREDITS

(Images used under license from Shutterstock.com)

Fabric Rolls, page 6 (contributor: Vladeep)
Alpaca, page 10 (contributor: Irine and Andrew)
Angora, page 10 (contributor: minianne)
Silk, page 10 (contributor: Natalya Vdovina)
Wool, page 10 (contributor: junjunalex)
Mohair, page 10 (contributor: Olirina)
Cashmere, page 10 (contributor: New Africa)
Cotton, page 11 (contributor: photo_jeongh)
Linen, page 11 (contributor: Agnes Kantaruk)
Jute, page 11 (contributor: gustavomellossa)
Hemp, page 11 (contributor: 7th Son Studio)
Ramie, page 11 (contributor: maewshooter)
Rayon, page 12 (contributor: Stanley Kalvan)
Tencel, page 12 (contributor: Fascinadora)
Acetate, page 12 (contributor: Stanley Kalvan)
Nylon, page 12 (contributor: Kwangmoozaa)
Polyester, page 12 (contributor: Evannovostro)
Elastane, page 12 (contributor: Aki 2007)
Acrylic, page 12 (contributor: Zuzha)
Corduroy, page 20 (contributor: all I like)
Faux Fur, page 20 (contributor: Darren Whittingham)
Velcro, page 20 (contributor: Daniel Brasil)
Interfacing, page 21 (contributor: Kitreel)
Felt, Page 21 (contributor: (ivan_kislitsin)
Leather, Page 21 (contributor: Wongsakorn Dulyavit)
Fiberfill, page 21 (contributor: Yelni Widiya)
Organza, page 25 (contributor: severija)
Regular Gauze, page 25 (contributor: Vlad Antonov)
Double Gauze, page 25 (contributor: Chanitada)
Taffeta, page 27 (contributor: PhotoMavenStock)
Eyelet, page 27 (contributor: APugach)
Shantung, page 27 (contributor: quirkychick)
Velvet, page 27 (contributor: Chinnapong)
Corduroy, page 27 (contributor: V_Sot_Visual_Content)
Twill, page 29 (contributor: Kyle_Yoon)
Mikado, page 29 (contributor: Imagentle)
Denim, page 29 (contributor: Dmitriy Sobitnyak)
Chambray, page 29 (contributor: Ohleaf)
Pinstripe, page 29 (contributor: J. Helgason)
Plaid, page 29 (contributor: striped_doll)
Gingham, page 29 (contributor: ThomasLENNE)
Houndstooth, page 29 (contributor: Kellis)
Glen Plaid, page 31 (contributor: Belle Hung)
Argyle, page 31 (contributor: Elisa Galceran Garcia)
Herringbone, page 31 (contributor: Supergrey)
Jacquard, page 31 (contributor: Shkind)
Damask, page 31 (contributor: Dario Pena)
Ribbed, page 31 (contributor: Svetlana Zhukova)
Piqué, page 31 (contributor: ArtKio)
Spandex, page 33 (contributor: Lili.Q)
Fleece, page 33 (contributor: fotolyubitel)
Mesh, page 33 (contributor: prapann)
Velour, page 33 (contributor: Chinnapong)
Quilted, page 33 (contributor: M.Photos)
Flock, page 33 (contributor: James Jeong)
Tulle, page 33 (contributor: Ortis)
Lace, page 33 (contributor: Ruslan Kudrin)
Bias Tape, page 34 (contributor: Lyudmila Epova)
Camouflage, page 35 (contributor: DONOT6_STUDIO)
Chevron, page 35 (contributor: Lava 4 images)
Paisley, page 35 (contributor: Sergei Mishchenko)
Polka dots, page 35 (contributor: Tarzhanova)
Stripes, page 35 (contributor: everydayplus)
Tie Dye, page 35 (contributor: P-fotography)
Floral, page 35 (contributor: Irina_raduga)
Ikat, page 35 (contributor: Cholpan)
Nylon Coil, page 37 (contributor: Butus)
Invisible Zipper, page 37 (contributor: Paket)
Metal Chain, page 37 (contributor: Butus)
Plastic Molded, page 37 (contributor: Butus)
Sewing Machine, page 45 (contributor: Ivan Zhurba)
Dress Forms, page 61 (contributor: Retan)
Measurement, page 71 (contributor: MIND AND I)

INDEX

G

H

I

J

K

Y

Z